Management of Change

MANAGEMENT OF CHANGE

A Harvard Business Review Paperback

Harvard Business Review paperback No. 90064

The *Harvard Business Review* articles in this collection
are available individually. Discounts apply to quantity
purchases. For information and ordering, contact Operations Department, Harvard Business School Publishing
Division, Boston, MA 02163. Telephone: (617) 495-6192.
Fax: (617) 495-6985.

Editor's Note: Some articles included in this book may have
been written before authors and editors began to take into
consideration the role of women in management. We hope
the archaic usage representing all managers as male does not
detract from the usefulness of the collection.

Contents

New Directions
for Change

THE COMING OF THE NEW ORGANIZATION

by PETER F. DRUCKER

The typical large business 20 years hence will have fewer than half the levels of management of its counterpart today, and no more than a third the managers. In its structure, and in its management problems and concerns, it will bear little resemblance to the typical manufacturing company, circa 1950, which our textbooks still consider the norm. Instead it is far more likely to resemble organizations that neither the practicing manager nor the management scholar pays much attention to today: the hospital, the university, the symphony orchestra. For like them, the typical business will be knowledge-based, an organization composed largely of specialists who direct and discipline their own performance through organized feedback from colleagues, customers, and headquarters. For this reason, it will be what I call an information-based organization.

Businesses, especially large ones, have little choice but to become information-based. Demographics, for one, demands the shift. The center of gravity in employment is moving fast from manual and clerical workers to knowledge workers who resist the command-and-control model that business took from the military 100 years ago. Economics also dictates change, especially the need for large businesses to innovate and to be entrepreneurs. But above all, information technology demands the shift.

Advanced data-processing technology isn't necessary to create an information-based organization, of course. As we shall see, the British built just such an organization in India when "information technology" meant the quill pen, and barefoot runners were the "telecommunications" systems. But as advanced technology becomes more and more prevalent, we have to engage in analysis and

The large business 20 years hence is more likely to resemble a hospital or a symphony than a typical manufacturing company.

Peter F. Drucker is Marie Rankin Clarke Professor of Social Sciences and Management at the Claremont Graduate School, which recently named its management center after him. Widely known for his work on management practice and thought, he is the author of numerous articles and books, the most recent of which is The Frontiers of Management *(E.P. Dutton/Truman Talley Books, 1986). This is Mr. Drucker's twenty-fourth contribution to HBR.*

diagnosis—that is, in "information"—even more intensively or risk being swamped by the data we generate.

So far most computer users still use the new technology only to do faster what they have always done before, crunch conventional numbers. But as soon as a company takes the first tentative steps from data to information, its decision processes, management structure, and even the way its work gets done begin to be transformed. In fact, this is already happening, quite fast, in a number of companies throughout the world.

We can readily see the first step in this transformation process when we consider the impact of computer technology on capital-investment decisions. We have known for a long time that there is no one right way to analyze a proposed capital investment. To understand it we need at least six analyses: the expected rate of return; the payout period and the investment's expected productive life; the discounted present value of all returns through the productive lifetime of the investment; the risk in not making the investment or deferring it; the cost and risk in case of failure; and finally, the opportunity cost. Every accounting student is taught these concepts. But before the advent of data-processing capacity, the actual analyses would have taken man-years of clerical toil to complete. Now anyone with a spreadsheet should be able to do them in a few hours.

The availability of this information transforms the capital-investment analysis from opinion into diagnosis, that is, into the rational weighing of alternative assumptions. Then the information transforms the capital-investment decision from an opportunistic, financial decision governed by the numbers into a business decision based on the probability of alternative strategic assumptions. So the decision both presupposes a business strategy and challenges that strategy and its assumptions. What was once a budget exercise becomes an analysis of policy.

Information transforms a budget exercise into an analysis of policy.

The second area that is affected when a company focuses its data-processing capacity on producing information is its organization structure. Almost immediately, it becomes clear that both the number of management levels and the number of managers can be sharply cut. The reason is straightforward: it turns out that whole layers of management neither make decisions nor lead. Instead, their main, if not their only, function is to serve as "relays"—human boosters for the faint, unfocused signals that pass for communication in the traditional pre-information organization.

One of America's largest defense contractors made this discovery when it asked what information its top corporate and operating managers needed to do their jobs. Where did it come from? What form was it in? How did it flow? The search for answers soon revealed that whole layers of management—perhaps as many as 6 out of a total of 14—existed only because these questions had not been asked before. The company had had data galore. But it had always used its copious data for control rather than for information.

Information is data endowed with relevance and purpose. Converting data into information thus requires knowledge. And knowledge, by definition. is specialized. (In fact, truly knowledgeable people tend toward overspecialization, whatever their field, precisely because there is always so much more to know.)

The information-based organization requires far more specialists overall than the command-and-control companies we are accustomed to. Moreover, the specialists are found in operations, not at corporate headquarters. Indeed, the operating organization tends to become an organization of specialists of all kinds.

Information-based organizations need central operating work such as legal counsel, public relations, and labor relations as much as ever. But the need for service staffs—that is, for people without operating responsibilities who only advise, counsel, or coordinate—shrinks drastically. In its *central* management, the information-based organization needs few, if any, specialists.

Because of its flatter structure, the large, information-based organization will more closely resemble the businesses of a century ago than today's big companies. Back then, however, all the knowledge, such as it was, lay with the very top people. The rest were helpers or hands, who mostly did the same work and did as they were told. In the information-based organization, the knowledge will be primarily at the bottom, in the minds of the specialists who do different work and direct themselves. So today's typical organization in which knowledge tends to be concentrated in service staffs, perched rather insecurely between top management and the operating people, will likely be labeled a phase, an attempt to infuse knowledge from the top rather than obtain information from below.

Finally, a good deal of work will be done differently in the information-based organization. Traditional departments will serve as guardians of standards, as centers for training and the assignment of specialists; they won't be where the work gets done. That will happen largely in task-focused teams.

This change is already under way in what used to be the most clearly defined of all departments—research. In pharmaceuticals, in telecommunications, in papermaking, the traditional *sequence* of research, development, manufacturing, and marketing is being replaced by *synchrony*: specialists from all these functions work together as a team, from the inception of research to a product's establishment in the market.

How task forces will develop to tackle other business opportunities and problems remains to be seen. I suspect, however, that the need for a task force, its assignment, its composition, and its leadership will have to be decided on case by case. So the organization that will be developed will go beyond the matrix and may indeed be quite different from it. One thing is clear, though: it will require greater self-discipline and even greater emphasis on individual responsibility for relationships and for communications.

Traditional departments won't be where the work gets done.

To say that information technology is transforming business enterprises is simple. What this transformation will require of companies and top managements is much harder to decipher. That is why I find it helpful to look for clues in other kinds of information-based organizations, such as the hospital, the symphony orchestra, and the British administration in India.

A fair-sized hospital of about 400 beds will have a staff of several hundred physicians and 1,200 to 1,500 paramedics divided among some 60 medical and paramedical specialities. Each specialty has its own knowledge, its own training, its own language. In each specialty, especially the paramedical ones like the clinical lab and physical therapy, there is a head person who is a working specialist rather than a full-time manager. The head of each specialty reports directly to the top, and there is little middle management. A good deal of the work is done in ad hoc teams as required by an individual patient's diagnosis and condition.

A large symphony orchestra is even more instructive, since for some works there may be a few hundred musicians on stage playing together. According to organization theory then, there should be several group vice president conductors and perhaps a half-dozen division VP conductors. But that's not how it works. There is only the conductor-CEO—and every one of the musicians plays directly to that person without an intermediary. And each is a high-grade specialist, indeed an artist.

But the best example of a large and successful information-based organization, and one without any middle management at all, is the British civil administration in India.[1]

The British ran the Indian subcontinent for 200 years, from the middle of the eighteenth century through World War II, without making any fundamental changes in organization structure or administrative policy. The Indian civil service never had more than 1,000 members to administer the vast and densely populated subcontinent—a tiny fraction (at most 1%) of the legions of Confucian mandarins and palace eunuchs employed next door to administer a not-much-more populous China. Most of the Britishers were quite young; a 30-year-old was a survivor, especially in the early years. Most lived alone in isolated outposts with the nearest countryman a day or two of travel away, and for the first hundred years there was no telegraph or railroad.

The organization structure was totally flat. Each district officer reported directly to the "Coo," the provincial political secretary. And since there were nine provinces, each political secretary had at least 100 people reporting directly to him, many times what the doctrine of the span of control would allow. Nevertheless, the system worked remarkably well, in large part because it was designed to ensure that each of its members had the information he needed to do his job.

Each month the district officer spent a whole day writing a full report to the political secretary in the provincial capital. He discussed each of his principal tasks—there were only four, each clearly delineated. He put down in detail what he had expected would happen with respect to each of them, what actually did happen, and why, if there was a discrepancy, the two differed. Then he wrote down what he expected would happen in the ensuing month with respect to each key task and what he was going to do about it, asked questions about policy, and commented on long-term opportunities, threats, and needs. In turn, the political secretary "minuted" every one of those reports—that is, he wrote back a full comment.

The best example of a large and successful information-based organization had no middle management at all.

---

1. The standard account is Philip Woodruff, *The Men Who Ruled India*, especially the first volume, *The Founders of Modern India* (New York: St. Martin's, 1954). How the system worked day by day is charmingly told in *Sowing* (New York: Harcourt Brace Jovanovich, 1962), volume one of the autobiography of Leonard Woolf (Virginia Woolf's husband).

On the basis of these examples, what can we say about the requirements of the information-based organization? And what are its management problems likely to be? Let's look first at the requirements. Several hundred musicians and their CEO, the conductor, can play together because they all have the same score. It tells both flutist and timpanist what to play and when. And it tells the conductor what to expect from each and when. Similarly, all the specialists in the hospital share a common mission: the care and cure of the sick. The diagnosis is their "score"; it dictates specific action for the X-ray lab, the dietitian, the physical therapist, and the rest of the medical team.

Information-based organizations, in other words, require clear, simple, common objectives that translate into particular actions. At the same time, however, as these examples indicate, information-based organizations also need concentration on one objective or, at most, on a few.

Because the "players" in an information-based organization are specialists, they cannot be told how to do their work. There are probably few orchestra conductors who could coax even one note out of a French horn, let alone show the horn player how to do it. But the conductor can focus the horn player's skill and knowledge on the musicians' joint performance. And this focus is what the leaders of an information-based business must be able to achieve.

Yet a business has no "score" to play by except the score it writes as it plays. And whereas neither a first-rate performance of a symphony nor a miserable one will change what the composer wrote, the performance of a business continually creates new and different scores against which its performance is assessed. So an information-based business must be structured around goals that clearly state management's performance expectations for the enterprise and for each part and specialist and around organized feedback that compares results with these performance expectations so that every member can exercise self-control.

The other requirement of an information-based organization is that everyone take information responsibility. The bassoonist in the orchestra does so every time she plays a note. Doctors and paramedics work with an elaborate system of reports and an information center, the nurse's station on the patient's floor. The district officer in India acted on this responsibility every time he filed a report.

The key to such a system is that everyone asks: Who in this organization depends on me for what information? And on whom, in turn, do I depend? Each person's list will always include superiors and subordinates. But the most important names on it will be those of colleagues, people with whom one's primary relationship is coordination. The relationship of the internist, the surgeon, and the anesthesiologist is one example. But the relationship of a biochemist, a pharmacologist, the medical director in charge of clinical testing, and a marketing specialist in a pharmaceutical company is no different. It, too, requires each party to take the fullest information responsibility.

Information responsibility to others is increasingly understood, especially in middle-sized companies. But information responsibility to oneself is still largely neglected. That is, everyone in an organization should constantly be thinking through what information he or she needs to do the job and to make a contribution.

Who depends on me for information? And on whom do I depend?

This may well be the most radical break with the way even the most highly computerized businesses are still being run today. There, people either assume the more data, the more information—which was a perfectly valid assumption yesterday when data were scarce, but leads to data overload and information blackout now that they are plentiful. Or they believe that information specialists know what data executives and professionals need in order to have information. But information specialists are tool makers. They can tell us what tool to use to hammer upholstery nails into a chair. We need to decide whether we should be upholstering a chair at all.

Executives and professional specialists need to think through what information is for them, what data they need: first, to know what they are doing; then, to be able to decide what they should be doing; and finally, to appraise how well they are doing. Until this happens MIS departments are likely to remain cost centers rather than become the result centers they could be.

Most large businesses have little in common with the examples we have been looking at. Yet to remain competitive—maybe even to survive—they will have to convert themselves into information-based organizations, and fairly quickly. They will have to change old habits and acquire new ones. And the more successful a company has been, the more difficult and painful this process is apt to be. It will threaten the jobs, status, and opportunities of a good many people in the organization, especially the long-serving, middle-aged people in middle management who tend to be the least mobile and to feel most secure in their work, their positions, their relationships, and their behavior.

The information-based organization will also pose its own special management problems. I see as particularly critical:

1. Developing rewards, recognition, and career opportunities for specialists.
2. Creating unified vision in an organization of specialists.
3. Devising the management structure for an organization of task forces.
4. Ensuring the supply, preparation, and testing of top management people.

To remain competitive—maybe even to survive—businesses will have to convert themselves into organizations of knowledgeable specialists.

Bassoonists presumably neither want nor expect to be anything but bassoonists. Their career opportunities consist of moving from second bassoon to first bassoon and perhaps of moving from a second-rank orchestra to a better, more prestigious one. Similarly, many medical technologists neither expect nor want to be anything but medical technologists. Their career opportunities consist of a fairly good chance of moving up to senior technician, and a very slim chance of becoming lab director. For those who make it to lab director, about 1 out of every 25 or 30 technicians, there is also the opportunity to move to a bigger, richer hospital. The district officer in India had practically no chance for professional growth except possibly to be relocated, after a three-year stint, to a bigger district.

Opportunities for specialists in an information-based business organization should be more plentiful than they are in an orchestra or hospital, let alone in the Indian civil service. But as in these organizations, they will primarily be opportunities for advancement within the specialty, and for limited advancement at that. Advancement into "management" will be the exception, for the simple reason that there will be far fewer middle-management positions to move into. This contrasts sharply with the traditional organization where, except in the research lab, the main line of advancement in rank is out of the specialty and into general management.

More than 30 years ago General Electric tackled this problem by creating "parallel opportunities" for "individual professional contributors." Many companies have followed this example. But professional specialists themselves have largely rejected it as a solution. To them—and to their management colleagues—the only meaningful opportunities are promotions into management. And the prevailing compensation structure in practically all businesses reinforces this attitude because it is heavily biased towards managerial positions and titles.

There are no easy answers to this problem. Some help may come from looking at large law and consulting firms, where even the most senior partners tend to be specialists, and associates who will not make partner are outplaced fairly early on. But whatever scheme is eventually developed will work only if the values and compensation structure of business are drastically changed.

The second challenge that management faces is giving its organization of specialists a common vision, a view of the whole.

In the Indian civil service, the district officer was expected to see the "whole" of his district. But to enable him to concentrate on it, the government services that arose one after the other in the nineteenth century (forestry, irrigation, the archaeological survey, public health and sanitation, roads) were organized outside the administrative structure, and had virtually no contact with the district officer. This meant that the district officer became increasingly isolated from the activities that often had the greatest impact on—and the greatest importance for—his district. In the end, only the provincial government or the central government in Delhi had a view of the "whole," and it was an increasingly abstract one at that.

A business simply cannot function this way. It needs a view of the whole and a focus on the whole to be shared among a great many of its professional specialists, certainly among the senior ones. And yet it will have to accept, indeed will have to foster, the pride and professionalism of its specialists—if only because, in the absence of opportunities to move into middle management, their motivation must come from that pride and professionalism.

One way to foster professionalism, of course, is through assignments to task forces. And the information-based business will use more and more smaller self-governing units, assigning them tasks tidy enough for "a good man to get his arms around," as the old phrase has it. But to what extent should information-based businesses rotate performing specialists out of their specialties and into new ones? And to what extent will top management have to accept as its top priority making and maintaining a common vision across professional specialties?

Heavy reliance on task-force teams assuages one problem. But it aggravates another: the management structure of the information-based organization. Who will the business's managers be? Will they be task-force leaders? Or will there be a two-headed monster—a specialist structure, comparable, perhaps, to the way attending physi-

Who will the business's managers be?

cians function in a hospital, and an administrative structure of task-force leaders?

The decisions we face on the role and function of the task-force leaders are risky and controversial. Is theirs a permanent assignment, analagous to the job of the supervisory nurse in the hospital? Or is it a function of the task that changes as the task does? Is it an assignment or a position? Does it carry any rank at all? And if it does, will the task-force leaders become in time what the product managers have been at Procter & Gamble: the basic units of management and the company's field officers? Might the task-force leaders eventually replace department heads and vice presidents?

Signs of every one of these developments exist, but there is neither a clear trend nor much understanding as to what each entails. Yet each would give rise to a different organizational structure from any we are familiar with.

Finally, the toughest problem will probably be to ensure the supply, preparation, and testing of top management people. This is, of course, an old and central dilemma as well as a major reason for the general acceptance of decentralization in large businesses in the last 40 years. But the existing business organization has a great many middle-management positions that are supposed to prepare and test a person. As a result, there are usually a good many people to choose from when filling a senior management slot. With the number of middle-management positions sharply cut, where will the information-based organization's top executives come from? What will be their preparation? How will they have been tested?

Decentralization into autonomous units will surely be even more critical than it is now. Perhaps we will even copy the German *Gruppe* in which the decentralized units are set up as separate companies with their own top managements. The Germans use this model precisely because of their tradition of promoting people in their specialties, especially in research and engineering; if they did not have available commands in near-independent subsidiaries to put people in, they would have little opportunity to train and test their most promising professionals. These subsidiaries are thus somewhat like the farm teams of a major-league baseball club.

We may also find that more and more top management jobs in big companies are filled by hiring people away from smaller companies. This is the way that major orchestras get their conductors – a young conductor earns his or her spurs in a small orchestra or opera house, only to be hired away by a larger one. And the heads of a good many large hospitals have had similar careers.

Can business follow the example of the orchestra and hospital where top management has become a separate career? Conductors and hospital administrators come out of courses in conducting or schools of hospital administration respectively. We see something of this sort in France, where large companies are often run by men who have spent their entire previous careers in government service. But in most countries this would be unacceptable to the organization (only France has the *mystique* of the *grandes écoles*). And even in France, businesses, especially large ones, are becoming too demanding to be run by people without firsthand experience and a proven success record.

Thus the entire top management process – preparation, testing, succession – will become even more problematic than it already is.

With middle management sharply cut, where will the top executives come from?

There will be a growing need for experienced businesspeople to go back to school. And business schools will surely need to work out what successful professional specialists must know to prepare themselves for high-level positions as *business* executives and *business* leaders.

Since modern business enterprise first arose, after the Civil War in the United States and the Franco-Prussian War in Europe, there have been two major evolutions in the concept and structure of organizations. The first took place in the ten years between 1895 and 1905. It distinguished management from ownership and established management as work and task in its own right. This happened first in Germany, when Georg Siemens, the founder and head of Germany's premier bank, *Deutsche Bank*, saved the electrical apparatus company his cousin Werner had founded after Werner's sons and heirs had mismanaged it into near collapse. By threatening to cut off the bank's loans, he forced his cousins to turn the company's management over to professionals. A little later, J.P. Morgan, Andrew Carnegie, and John D. Rockefeller, Sr. followed suit in their massive restructurings of U.S. railroads and industries.

The second evolutionary change took place 20 years later. The development of what we still see as the modern corporation began with Pierre S. du Pont's restructuring of his family company in the early twenties and continued with Alfred P. Sloan's redesign of General Motors a few years later. This introduced the command-and-control organization of today, with its emphasis on decentralization, central service staffs, personnel management, the whole apparatus of budgets and controls, and the important distinction between policy and operations. This stage culminated in the massive reorganization of General Electric in the early 1950s, an action that perfected the model most big businesses around the world (including Japanese organizations) still follow.[2]

Now we are entering a third period of change: the shift from the command-and-control organization, the organization of departments and divisions, to the information-based organization, the organization of knowledge specialists. We can perceive, though perhaps only dimly, what this organization will look like. We can identify some of its main characteristics and requirements. We can point to central problems of values, structure, and behavior. But the job of actually building the information-based organization is still ahead of us—it is the managerial challenge of the future. ▽

Reprint 88105

We can identify requirements and point to problems; the job of building is still ahead.

---

2. Alfred D. Chandler, Jr. has masterfully chronicled the process in his two books *Strategy and Structure* (Cambridge: MIT Press, 1962) and *The Visible Hand* (Cambridge: Harvard University Press, 1977)—surely the best studies of the administrative history of any major institution. The process itself and its results were presented and analyzed in two of my books: *The Concept of the Corporation* (New York: John Day, 1946) and *The Practice of Management* (New York: Harper Brothers, 1954).

The New Managerial Work

by Rosabeth Moss Kanter

Managerial work is undergoing such enormous and rapid change that many managers are reinventing their profession as they go. With little precedent to guide them, they are watching hierarchy fade away and the clear distinctions of title, task, department, even corporation, blur. Faced with extraordinary levels of complexity and interdependency, they watch traditional sources of power erode and the old motivational tools lose their magic.

The cause is obvious. Competitive pressures are forcing corporations to adopt new flexible strategies and structures. Many of these are familiar: acquisitions and divestitures aimed at more focused combinations of business activities, reductions in management staff and levels of hierarchy, increased use of performance-based rewards. Other strategies are less common but have an even more profound effect. In a growing number of companies, for example, horizontal ties between peers are replacing vertical ties as channels of activity and communication. Companies are asking corporate staffs and functional departments to play a more strategic role with greater cross-departmental collaboration. Some orga-

Rosabeth Moss Kanter holds the Class of 1960 Chair as Professor of Business Administration at the Harvard Business School and concentrates on innovation and entrepreneurship in established companies. Her most recent book is When Giants Learn to Dance: Mastering the Challenges of Strategy, Management, and Careers in the 1990s (Simon & Schuster, 1989).

nizations are turning themselves nearly inside out –buying formerly internal services from outside suppliers, forming strategic alliances and supplier-customer partnerships that bring external relationships inside where they can influence company policy and practice. I call these emerging practices "postentrepreneurial" because they involve the application of entrepreneurial creativity and flexibility to established businesses.

Such changes come highly recommended by the experts who urge organizations to become leaner, less bureaucratic, more entrepreneurial. But so far, theorists have given scant attention to the dramatically altered realities of managerial work in these transformed corporations. We don't even have good words to describe the new relationships. "Superiors" and "subordinates" hardly seem accurate, and even "bosses" and "their people" imply more control and ownership than managers today actually possess. On top of it all, career paths are no longer straightforward and predictable but have become idiosyncratic and confusing.

Some managers experience the new managerial work as a loss of power because much of their authority used to come from hierarchical position. Now that everything seems negotiable by everyone, they are confused about how to mobilize and motivate staff. For other managers, the shift in roles and tasks offers greater personal power. The following case histories illustrate the responses of three managers in

The New Managerial Quandaries

■ At American Express, the CEO instituted a program called "One Enterprise" to encourage collaboration between different lines of business. One Enterprise has led to a range of projects where peers from different divisions work together on such synergistic ventures as cross-marketing, joint purchasing, and cooperative product and market innovation. Employees' rewards are tied to their One Enterprise efforts. Executives set goals and can earn bonuses for their contributions to results in other divisions.
□ But how do department managers control their people when they're working on cross-departmental teams? And who determines the size of the rewards when the interests of more than one area are involved?

■ At Security Pacific National Bank, internal departments have become forces in the external marketplace. For example, the bank is involved in a joint venture with local auto dealers to sell fast financing for car purchases. And the MIS department is now a profit center selling its services inside and outside the bank.
□ But what is the role of bank managers accountable for the success of such entrepreneurial ventures? And how do they shift their orientation from the role of boss in a chain of command to the role of customer?

■ At Digital Equipment Corporation, emphasis on supplier partnerships to improve quality and innovation has multiplied the need for cross-functional as well as cross-company collaboration. Key suppliers are included on product planning teams with engineering, manufacturing, and purchasing staff. Digital uses its human resources staff to train and do performance appraisals of its suppliers, as if they were part of the company. In cases where suppliers are also customers, purchasing and marketing departments also need to work collaboratively.
□ But how do managers learn enough about other functions to be credible, let alone influential, members of such teams? How do they maintain adequate communication externally while staying on top of what their own departments are doing? And how do they handle the extra work of responding to projects initiated by other areas?

■ At Banc One, a growing reliance on project teams spanning more than 70 affiliated banks has led the CEO to propose eliminating officer titles because of the lack of correlation between status as measured by title and status within the collaborative team.
□ But then what do "rank" and "hierarchy" mean anymore, especially for people whose careers consist of a sequence of projects rather than a sequence of promotions? What does "career" mean? Does it have a shape? Is there a ladder?

■ At Alcan, which is trying to find new uses and applications for its core product, aluminum, managers and professionals from line divisions form screening teams to consider and refine new-venture proposals. A venture manager, chosen from the screening team, takes charge of concepts that pass muster, drawing on Alcan's worldwide resources to build the new business. In one case of global synergy, Alcan created a new product for the Japanese market using Swedish and American technology and Canadian manufacturing capacity.
□ But why should senior managers release staff to serve on screening and project teams for new businesses when their own businesses are making do with fewer and fewer people? How do functionally oriented managers learn enough about worldwide developments to know when they might have something of value to offer someplace else? And how do the managers of these new ventures ever go back to the conventional line organization as middle managers once their venture has been folded into an established division?

■ At IBM, an emphasis on customer partnerships to rebuild market share is leading to practices quite new to the company. In some cases, IBM has formed joint development teams with customers, where engineers from both companies share proprietary data. In others, the company has gone beyond selling equipment to actually managing a customer's management information system. Eastman Kodak has handed its U.S. data center operations to IBM to consolidate and manage, which means lower fixed costs for Kodak and a greater ability to focus on its core businesses rather than on ancillary services. Some 300 former Kodak people still fill Kodak's needs as IBM employees, while two committees of IBM and Kodak managers oversee the partnership.
□ But who exactly do the data center people work for? Who is in charge? And how do traditional notions of managerial authority square with such a complicated set of relationships?

three different industries to the opportunities and dilemmas of structural change.

Hank is vice president and chief engineer for a leading heavy equipment manufacturer that is moving aggressively against foreign competition. One of the company's top priorities has been to increase the speed, quality, and cost-effectiveness of product development. So Hank worked with consultants to improve collaboration between manufacturing and other functions and to create closer alliances between the company and its outside suppliers. Gradually, a highly segmented operation became an integrated process involving project teams drawn from component divisions, functional departments, and external suppliers. But along the way, there were several unusual side effects. Different areas of responsibility overlapped. Some technical and manufacturing people were co-located. Liaisons from functional areas joined the larger development teams. Most unusual of all, project teams had a lot of direct contact with higher levels of the company.

Many of the managers reporting to Hank felt these changes as a loss of power. They didn't always know what their people were doing, but they still believed they ought to know. They no longer had sole input into performance appraisals; other people from other

> # New strategies challenge the old power of managers and shake hierarchy to its roots.

functions had a voice as well, and some of them knew more about employees' project performance. New career paths made it less important to please direct superiors in order to move up the functional line.

Moreover, employees often bypassed Hank's managers and interacted directly with decision makers inside and outside the company. Some of these so-called subordinates had contact with division executives and senior corporate staff, and sometimes they sat in on high-level strategy meetings to which their managers were not invited.

At first Hank thought his managers' resistance to the new process was just the normal noise associated with any change. Then he began to realize that something more profound was going on. The reorganization was challenging traditional notions about the role and power of managers and shaking traditional hierarchy to its roots. And no one could see what was taking its place.

When George became head of a major corporate department in a large bank holding company, he thought he had arrived. His title and rank were unmistakable, and his department was responsible for determining product-line policy for hundreds of bank branches and the virtual clerks–in George's eyes–who managed them. George staffed his department with MBAs and promised them rapid promotion.

Then the sand seemed to shift beneath him. Losing market position for the first time in recent memory, the bank decided to emphasize direct customer service at the branches. The people George considered clerks began to depart from George's standard policies and to tailor their services to local market conditions. In many cases, they actually demanded services and responses from George's staff, and the results of their requests began to figure in performance reviews of George's department. George's people were spending more and more time in the field with branch managers, and the corporate personnel department was even trying to assign some of George's MBAs to branch and regional posts.

To complicate matters, the bank's strategy included a growing role for technology. George felt that because he had no direct control over the information systems department, he should not be held fully accountable for every facet of product design and implementation. But fully accountable he was. He had to deploy people to learn the new technology and figure out how to work with it. Furthermore, the bank was asking product departments like George's to find ways to link existing products or develop new ones that crossed traditional categories. So George's people were often away on cross-departmental teams just when he wanted them for some internal assignment.

Instead of presiding over a tidy empire the way his predecessor had, George presided over what looked to him like chaos. The bank said senior executives should be "leaders, not managers," but George didn't know what that meant, especially since he seemed to have lost control over his subordinates' assignments, activities, rewards, and careers. He resented his perceived loss of status.

The CEO tried to show him that good results achieved the new way would bring great monetary rewards, thanks to a performance-based bonus program that was gradually replacing more modest yearly raises. But the pressures on George were also greater, unlike anything he'd ever experienced.

For Sally, purchasing manager at an innovative computer company, a new organizational strategy was a gain rather than a loss, although it changed her relationship with the people reporting to her. Less than ten years out of college, she was hired as an analyst–a semiprofessional, semiclerical job–then promoted to a purchasing manager's job in a sleepy staff department. She didn't expect to go much further in what was then a well-established hierarchy. But after a shocking downturn, top management encouraged employees to rethink traditional ways of doing things. Sally's boss, the head of purchasing, suggested that "partnerships" with key suppliers might improve quality, speed innovation, and reduce costs.

Soon Sally's backwater was at the center of policy-making, and Sally began to help shape strategy. She organized meetings between her company's senior executives and supplier CEOs. She sent her staff to contribute supplier intelligence at company semi-

In the new organization, it's hard to tell the managers from the nonmanagers.

nars on technical innovation, and she spent more of her own time with product designers and manufacturing planners. She led senior executives on a tour of supplier facilities, traveling with them in the corporate jet.

Because some suppliers were also important customers, Sally's staff began meeting frequently with marketing managers to share information and address joint problems. Sally and her group were now also acting as internal advocates for major suppliers. Furthermore, many of these external companies now contributed performance appraisals of Sally and her team, and their opinions weighed almost as heavily as those of her superiors.

As a result of the company's new direction, Sally felt more personal power and influence, and her ties to peers in other areas and to top management were stronger. But she no longer felt like a manager directing subordinates. Her staff had become a pool of resources deployed by many others besides Sally. She was exhilarated by her personal opportunities but not quite sure the people she managed should have the same freedom to choose their own assignments. After all, wasn't that a manager's prerogative?

Hank's, George's, and Sally's very different stories say much about the changing nature of managerial work. However hard it is for managers at the very top to remake strategy and structure, they themselves will probably retain their identity, status, and control. For the managers below them, structural change is often much harder. As work units become more participative and team oriented, and as professionals and knowledge workers become more prominent, the distinction between manager and nonmanager begins to erode.

To understand what managers must do to achieve results in the postentrepreneurial corporation, we need to look at the changing picture of how such companies operate. The picture has five elements:

1. There are a greater number and variety of channels for taking action and exerting influence.

2. Relationships of influence are shifting from the vertical to the horizontal, from chain of command to peer networks.

3. The distinction between managers and those managed is diminishing, especially in terms of information, control over assignments, and access to external relationships.

4. External relationships are increasingly important as sources of internal power and influence, even of career development.

5. As a result of the first four changes, career development has become less intelligible but also less circumscribed. There are fewer assured routes to success, which produces anxiety. At the same time, career paths are more open to innovation, which produces opportunity.

To help companies implement their competitive organizational strategies, managers must learn new ways to manage, confronting changes in their own bases of power and recognizing the need for new ways to motivate people.

The Bases of Power

The changes I've talked about can be scary for people like George and the managers reporting to Hank, who were trained to know their place, to follow orders, to let the company take care of their careers, to do things by the book. The book is gone. In the new corporation, managers have only themselves to count on for success. They must learn to operate without the crutch of hierarchy. Position, title, and authority are no longer adequate tools, not in a world where subordinates are encouraged to think for themselves and where managers have to work synergistically with other departments and even other companies. Success depends increasingly on tapping into sources of good ideas, on figuring out whose collaboration is needed to act on those ideas, on working with both to produce results. In short, the new managerial work implies very different ways of obtaining and using power.

The postentrepreneurial corporation is not only leaner and flatter, it also has many more channels for action. Cross-functional projects, business-unit joint ventures, labor-management forums, innovation funds that spawn activities outside mainstream budgets and reporting lines, strategic partnerships with suppliers or customers—these are all overlays on the traditional organization chart, strategic pathways that ignore the chain of command.

Their existence has several important implications. For one thing, they create more potential centers of power. As the ways to combine resources increase, the ability to command diminishes. Alternative paths of communication, resource access, and execution erode the authority of those in the nominal chain of command. In other words, the opportunity for greater speed and flexibility undermines hierarchy. As more and more strategic action takes place in these channels, the jobs that focus inward on particular departments decline in power.

As a result, the ability of managers to get things done depends more on the number of networks in which they're centrally involved than on their height in a hierarchy. Of course, power in any organization always has a network component, but rank and formal structure used to be more limiting. For example, access to information and the ability to get informal backing were often confined to the few officially sanctioned contact points between departments or between the company and its vendors or customers. Today these official barriers are disappearing, while so-called informal networks grow in importance.

In the emerging organization, managers add value by deal making, by brokering at interfaces, rather than by presiding over their individual empires. It was traditionally the job of top executives or specialists to scan the business environment for new ideas, opportunities, and resources. This kind of environmental scanning is now an important part of a manager's job at every level and in every function. And the environment to be scanned includes various company divisions, many potential outside partners, and large parts of the world. At the same time, people are encouraged to think about what they know that might have value elsewhere. An engineer designing windshield wipers, for example, might discover properties of rubber adhesion to glass that could be useful in other manufacturing areas.

Every manager must think cross-functionally because every department has to play a strategic role, understanding and contributing to other facets of the business. In Hank's company, the technical managers and staff working on design engineering used to concentrate only on their own areas of expertise. Under the new system, they have to keep in mind what manufacturing does and how it does it. They need to visit plants and build relationships so they can ask informed questions.

One multinational corporation, eager to extend the uses of its core product, put its R&D staff and lab-oratory personnel in direct contact with marketing experts to discuss lines of research. Similarly, the superior economic track record of Raytheon's New Products Center—dozens of new products and patents yielding profits many times their development costs—derives from the connections it builds between its inventors and the engineering and marketing staffs of the business units it serves.

This strategic and collaborative role is particularly important for the managers and professionals on corporate staffs. They need to serve as integrators and facilitators, not as watchdogs and interventionists. They need to sell their services, justify themselves to the business units they serve, literally compete with outside suppliers. General Foods recently put overhead charges for corporate staff services on a pay-as-you-use basis. Formerly, these charges were either assigned uniformly to users and nonusers alike, or the services were mandatory. Product managers sometimes had to work through as many as eight layers of management and corporate staff to get business

To add value, managers think and work across boundaries.

plans approved. Now these staffs must prove to the satisfaction of their internal customers that their services add value.

By contrast, some banks still have corporate training departments that do very little except get in the way. They do no actual training, for example, yet they still exercise veto power over urgent divisional training decisions and consultant contracts.

As managers and professionals spend more time working across boundaries with peers and partners over whom they have no direct control, their negotiating skills become essential assets. Alliances and partnerships transform impersonal, arm's-length contracts into relationships involving joint planning and joint decision making. Internal competitors and adversaries become allies on whom managers depend for their own success. At the same time, more managers at more levels are active in the kind of external diplomacy that only the CEO or selected staffs used to conduct.

In the collaborative forums that result, managers are more personally exposed. It is trust that makes partnerships work. Since collaborative ventures often bring together groups with different methods, cultures, symbols, even languages, good deal making depends on empathy—the ability to step into other people's shoes and appreciate their goals. This applies not only to intricate global joint ventures but also to the efforts of engineering and manufacturing to work together more effectively. Effective communication in a cooperative effort rests on more than a simple exchange of information; people must be adept at anticipating the responses of other groups. "Before I get too excited about our department's design ideas," an engineering manager told me, "I'm learning to ask myself, 'What's the marketing position on this? What

> ## Today's executive must bargain, negotiate, and sell ideas like any other politician.

will manufacturing say?' That sometimes forces me to make changes before I even talk to them."

An increase in the number of channels for strategic contact within the postentrepreneurial organization means more opportunities for people with ideas or information to trigger action: salespeople encouraging account managers to build strategic partnerships with customers, for example, or technicians searching for ways to tap new-venture funds to develop software. Moreover, top executives who have to spend more time on cross-boundary relationships are forced to delegate more responsibility to lower level managers. Delegation is one more blow to hierarchy, of course, since subordinates with greater responsibility are bolder about speaking up, challenging authority, and charting their own course.

For example, it is common for new-venture teams to complain publicly about corporate support departments and to reject their use in favor of external service providers, often to the consternation of more orthodox superiors. A more startling example occured in a health care company where members of a task force charged with finding synergies among three lines of business shocked corporate executives by criticizing upper management behavior in their report. Service on the task force had created collective awareness of a shared problem and had given people the courage to confront it.

The search for internal synergies, the development of strategic alliances, and the push for new ventures all emphasize the political side of a leader's work. Executives must be able to juggle a set of constituencies rather than control a set of subordinates. They have to bargain, negotiate, and sell instead of making unilateral decisions and issuing commands. The leader's task, as Chester Barnard recognized long ago, is to develop a network of cooperative relationships among all the people, groups, and organizations that have

something to contribute to an economic enterprise. Postentrepreneurial strategies magnify the complexity of this task. After leading Teknowledge, a producer of expert systems software, through development alliances with six corporations including General Motors and Procter & Gamble, company chairman Lee Hecht said he felt like the mayor of a small city. "I have a constituency that won't quit. It takes a hell of a lot of balancing." The kind of power achieved through a network of stakeholders is very different from the kind of power managers wield in a traditional bureaucracy. The new way gets more done, but it also takes more time. And it creates an illusion about freedom and security.

The absence of day-to-day constraints, the admonition to assume responsibility, the pretense of equality, the elimination of visible status markers, the prevalence of candid dialogues across hierarchical levels – these can give employees a false sense that all hierarchy is a thing of the past. Yet at the same time, employees still count on hierarchy to shield them when things go wrong. This combination would create the perfect marriage of freedom and support – freedom when people want to take risks, support when the risks don't work out.

In reality, less benevolent combinations are also possible, combinations not of freedom and support but of insecurity and loss of control. There is often a pretense in postentrepreneurial companies that sta-

> ## The promise of freedom has a dark side: insecurity and loss of control.

tus differences have nothing to do with power, that the deference paid to top executives derives from their superior qualifications rather than from the power they have over the fates of others. But the people at the top of the organization chart still wield power – and sometimes in ways that managers below them experience as arbitrary. Unprecedented individual freedom also applies to top managers, who are now free to make previously unimaginable deals, order unimaginable cuts, or launch unimaginable takeovers. The reorganizations that companies undertake in their search for new synergies can uncover the potential unpredictability and capriciousness of corporate careers. A man whose company was undergoing drastic restructuring told me, "For all of my ownership share and strategic centrality and voice in decisions, I can still be faced with a shift in direction not of my own making. I can still be reorganized into a corner. I can still be relocated into oblivion. I can still be reviewed out of my special project budget."

These realities of power, change, and job security are important because they affect the way people view their leaders. When the illusion of simultaneous freedom and protection fades, the result can be a loss of motivation.

Sources of Motivation

One of the essential, unchanging tasks of leaders is to motivate and guide performance. But motivational tools are changing fast. More and more businesses are doing away with the old bureaucratic incentives and using entrepreneurial opportunity to attract the best talent. Managers must exercise more leadership even as they watch their bureaucratic power slip away. Leadership, in short, is more difficult yet more critical than ever.

Because of the unpredictability of even the most benign restructuring, managers are less able to guarantee a particular job—or any job at all—no matter what a subordinate's performance level. The reduction in hierarchical levels curtails a manager's ability to promise promotion. New compensation systems that make bonuses and raises dependent on objective performance measures and on team appraisals deprive managers of their role as the sole arbiter of higher pay. Cross-functional and cross-company teams can rob managers of their right to direct or even understand the work their so-called subordinates do. In any case, the shift from routine work, which was amenable to oversight, to "knowledge" work, which often is not, erodes a manager's claim to superior expertise. And partnerships and ventures that put lower level people in direct contact with each other across departmental and company boundaries cut heavily into the managerial monopoly on information. At a consumer packaged-goods manufacturer that replaced several levels of hierarchy with teams, plant team members in direct contact with the sales force often had data on product ordering trends before the higher level brand managers who set product policy.

As if the loss of carrots and sticks was not enough, many managers can no longer even give their people clear job standards and easily mastered procedural rules. Postentrepreneurial corporations seek problem-solving, initiative-taking employees who will go the unexpected extra mile for the customer. To complicate the situation further still, the complexities of work in the new organization—projects and relationships clamoring for attention in every direction—exacerbate the feeling of overload.

With the old motivational tool kit depleted, leaders need new and more effective incentives to encourage high performance and build commitment. There are five new tools:

Mission. Helping people believe in the importance of their work is essential, especially when other forms of certainty and security have disappeared. Good leaders can inspire others with the power and excitement of their vision and give people a sense of purpose and pride in their work. Pride is often a better source of motivation than the traditional corporate career ladder and the promotion-based reward system. Technical professionals, for example, are often motivated most effectively by the desire to see their work contribute to an excellent final product.

Agenda Control. As career paths lose their certainty and companies' futures grow less predictable, people can at least be in charge of their own professional lives. More and more professionals are passing up jobs with glamour and prestige in favor of jobs that give them greater control over their own activities and direction. Leaders give their subordinates this opportunity when they give them release time to work on pet projects, when they emphasize results instead of procedures, and when they delegate work and the decisions about how to do it. Choice of their next project is a potent reward for people who perform well.

Share of Value Creation. Entrepreneurial incentives that give teams a piece of the action are highly appropriate in collaborative companies. Because extra rewards are based only on measurable results, this approach also conserves resources. Innovative companies are experimenting with incentives like phantom stock for development of new ventures and other strategic achievements, equity participation in project returns, and bonuses pegged to key performance targets. Given the cross-functional nature of many projects today, rewards of this kind must sometimes be systemwide, but individual managers can also ask for a bonus pool for their own areas, contingent, of course, on meeting performance goals. And everyone can share the kinds of rewards that are abundant and free—awards and recognition.

Learning. The chance to learn new skills or apply them in new arenas is an important motivator in a turbulent environment because it's oriented toward securing the future. "The learning organization" promises to become a 1990s business buzzword as companies seek to learn more systematically from their experience and to encourage continuous learning for their people. In the world of high technology, where people understand uncertainty, the attractiveness of any company often lies in its capacity to provide learning and experience. By this calculus, access to training, mentors, and challenging projects is more important than pay or benefits. Some prominent companies – General Electric, for example – have always been able to attract top talent, even when they could not promise upward mobility, because people see them as a training ground, a good place to learn, and a valuable addition to a résumé.

Reputation. Reputation is a key resource in professional careers, and the chance to enhance it can be an outstanding motivator. The professional's reliance on reputation stands in marked contrast to the bureaucrat's anonymity. Professionals have to make a name for themselves, while traditional corporate managers and employees stayed behind the scenes. Indeed, the accumulation of reputational "capital" provides not only an immediate ego boost but also the kind of publicity that can bring other rewards, even other job offers. Managers can enhance reputation – and improve motivation – by creating stars, by providing abundant public recognition and visible awards, by crediting the authors of innovation, by publicizing people outside their own departments, and by plugging people into organizational and professional networks.

The new, collaborative organization is predicated on a logic of flexible work assignments, not of fixed job responsibilities. To promote innovation and responsiveness, two of today's competitive imperatives, managers need to see this new organization as a

> When an engineer saw a TV ad for his design, he shouted to his family, "Hey! That's mine!" *That's* compensation.

cluster of activity sets, not as a rigid structure. The work of leadership in this new corporation will be to organize both sequential and synchronous projects of varying length and breadth, through which varying combinations of people will move, depending on the tasks, challenges, and opportunities facing the area and its partners at any given moment.

Leaders need to carve out projects with tangible accomplishments, milestones, and completion dates and then delegate responsibility for these projects to the people who flesh them out. Clearly delimited projects can counter overload by focusing effort and can provide short-term motivation when the fate of

the long-term mission is uncertain. Project responsibility leads to ownership of the results and sometimes substitutes for other forms of reward. In companies where product development teams define and run their own projects, members commonly say that the greatest compensation they get is seeing the advertisements for their products. "Hey, that's mine! I did that!" one engineer told me he trumpeted to his family the first time he saw a commercial for his group's innovation.

This sense of ownership, along with a definite time frame, can spur higher levels of effort. Whenever people are engaged in creative or problem-solving projects that will have tangible results by deadline dates, they tend to come in at all hours, to think about the project in their spare time, to invest in it vast sums of physical and emotional energy. Knowing that the project will end and that completion will be an occasion for reward and recognition makes it possible to work much harder.

Leaders in the new organization do not lack motivational tools, but the tools are different from those of traditional corporate bureaucrats. The new rewards are based not on status but on contribution, and they consist not of regular promotion and automatic pay raises but of excitement about mission and a share of the glory and the gains of success. The new security is not employment security (a guaranteed job no matter what) but *employability* security – increased value in the internal and external labor markets. Commitment to the organization still matters, but today managers build commitment by offering project opportunities. The new loyalty is not to the boss or to the company but to projects that actualize a mission and offer challenge, growth, and credit for results.

The old bases of managerial authority are eroding, and new tools of leadership are taking their place. Managers whose power derived from hierarchy and who were accustomed to a limited area of personal control are learning to shift their perspectives and widen their horizons. The new managerial work consists of looking outside a defined area of responsibility to sense opportunities and of forming project teams drawn from any relevant sphere to address them. It involves communication and collaboration across functions, across divisions, and across companies whose activities and resources overlap. Thus rank, title, or official charter will be less important factors in success at the new managerial work than having the knowledge, skills, and sensitivity to mobilize people and motivate them to do their best. ▽

*From one of America's most respected managers,
a State of the Union address.*

The State of American Management

by Walter B. Wriston

The state of American management today is good. I am not one of those people who believes that America is not "competitive." In fact, to me "competitive" is really just a code word for protection. I believe that American managers are part and parcel of the most dynamic economy in the world—and that American managers deserve a great deal of the credit for keeping that economy healthy and growing. Today we are in the seventh year of an unprecedented economic expansion—an expansion for which the classical economists have been lighting candles every quarter since I can remember.

But what they don't know or keep forgetting is the fundamental truth about the United States and its economy: this is the only country in the world that renews itself every day. All of the economists, all of the academics, all of the people who wring their hands over America's decline forget that coming off the boat down at the docks this morning were 25 Koreans, 150 Mexicans, 3 Hungarians, and many more. Go look at U.S. colleges today. The leading students, the brightest scholars are from China or Taiwan or practically anywhere on earth. All of us, except American Indians, originally came from somewhere else. The world is America's talent pool. The great genius of America is that it takes all these people from different places and somehow turns us all into

Americans. There is nowhere else like this—there has never been anything like it in the history of the world.

There is a second great advantage that America has over any other country in the world: this is the Age of Pluralism, and U.S. society is based on pluralism. There are thousands of different power centers in the United States; thousands of little companies on Route 128, in Silicon Valley, and spread across the

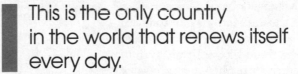

**This is the only country
in the world that renews itself
every day.**

country. And of course, there are the huge companies that have grown up over the last half-century. Between these two ends of the economy, there is enormous pressure—competing for the talent and intellectual horsepower that each end can attract and hold, for the products that each will produce, for political balance as each jockeys for recognition and ad-

Walter B. Wriston is a former chairman of Citicorp and Citibank and author of Risk and Other Four-Letter Words *(Harper & Row, 1986).*

vantage. These competing power centers are the expression of the uniquely American system; they are the vehicle through which U.S. managers contribute to their economy. And they shape the important changes that are going on in the practice of management—changes that will help keep managers and companies strong and competitive in the future.

Today the spirit of the entrepreneur has entered the mainstream of U.S. management. Entrepreneurship is transforming the corporate bureaucracy. And today we hear the word "management" less and the word "leadership" more. In the past, top managers were fascinated with finance and control: they dealt with secondary funding, adjustable preferreds, or they crunched the numbers sitting in the controller's bottom drawer.

Today a lot of the battles are won on the factory floor. And today more and more of U.S. industry consists of knowledge workers—people whose loyalty, whose affinity, is not to the old company logo but to doing the job right and contributing to how the work gets done. That means managers have to figure out how to motivate, coordinate, and conduct these collections of individuals, whether on the factory floor or in the office pools. It starts with articulating clear, limited goals about where the division or the company should go.

But even that has many different levels. Is the goal to continue on the trajectory that is on the best-fit curve right now? Or do you want to throw away 20% of your product line and use that money to concentrate on the other 80% of your products—products that represent the future? Do you want to make things the way you used to make them? Or are you convinced that you have to adopt a totally new approach in order to compete in the future?

Managers have always had to ask these questions. But today to be a leader, top executives need to be more like politicians than like the number-crunchers of yesterday. If there is a meter that measures the work of the manager, and at one end of the gauge are traditional management skills—all the technical information of finance, marketing, and the rest of the curriculum—and at the other end are leadership, goal setting, motivation, and articulation, then today the needle has swung from conducting monthly budget reviews to

articulating where the company is going, for what purpose, and how it's going to get there.

With this change in the work of the manager is coming a change in the shape of the organization. In well-run corporations, in the corporations that will survive and create the future, layers of management are disappearing. They are disappearing for two reasons: first, because micromanagement from the top is less important than inspiration, and second, because information flows to all levels of management, dispensing the same data at the same time to all. These changes make obsolete the extra layers of management—layers that once had to control and relay information. These managers would ask the people working under them what they were doing; then they would tell the people working above them what they said. They were transmission lines. But they spun not, neither did they weave; nor did they produce anything of added value. These are the layers that are coming out—and that need to come out.

They are coming out for still another reason, one that U.S. managers should have known all along but are learning now in company after company: the people who actually do a job,

The pace of knowledge is accelerating; it doubles every 10 to 12 years.

who are the closest to the work, know more about it than the manager. Today workers at all levels of the company are by definition knowledge workers. They have access to vital information, they take pride in their craft, and they understand things that no one else in the organization can.

I saw this firsthand 15 years ago, when New York City was close to bankruptcy and lacking funds to maintain roads and subway lines. The man who ran one of the public employees' unions was a friend of mine, and I remember when he told me, "The next subway wreck will be on the Coney Island line." I was astonished. "How do you know that?" I asked.

> The job of the manager today: find the best people you can, motivate them, and allow them to do the job their own way.

"It's easy," he said. "My guys maintain the tracks, and those tracks are in the worst shape of any in the system." Naturally I asked him, "Why don't you tell the manager?" His answer was a lesson for all of business. "Because," he told me, "management's priority is the big PERT chart, with its red, blue, and green dots. And on that chart, top management has decided to repair the E line going into Queens—and by the way, my guys tell me that line's in pretty good shape."

Not long ago, I saw how GE learned this lesson. One of its plants, which makes very complex machines, went on strike. To keep the plant running, the company brought in the supervisors who had designed the machines. They ran the factory beautifully, but after the strike was settled, they all said the same thing: "If I had actually worked the design out on this drill press instead of in my head, I could have made it better." The lesson is the same. Top managers have got to go back to basics and ask the people who have the problem, who have the skills, who have the hands-on knowledge, "How do you do it?"

There's another reason why this change is essential for U.S. managers—the accelerating pace of knowledge. It is a simple fact that roughly 85% of all the scientists who ever lived on this planet are alive today. Knowledge is doubling every 10 to 12 years. And as a result, the time between the realization of a brilliant idea and the delivery to the marketplace of a product based on that idea is the shortest it has ever been in history. It took almost 200 years for gunpowder to move from the laboratory to artillery. Today products can come out of the laboratory and be in the

marketplace in a few months. But for that to happen requires a different kind of management and organization than we have prided ourselves on in the past.

More than ever, it means talent. It means that every organization is more reliant on the talents of its people than ever before. Talent is the number one commodity in short supply. You can't have enough good people in your organization. Because the terrible truth is that good people can make bad systems work. And bad people can ruin even the best system. So the job of the manager today is very simple and very difficult: to find the best people you can, motivate them to do the job, and allow them to do it their own way. Interestingly, it's this description of the manager's job that is at the heart of the age we are entering, the Age of Restructuring. Whether it's the threat of global competition, the threat of the takeover, the threat of 1992, or just the fact that every so many years, industry, to survive, must restructure itself—U.S. managers no longer accept a business that is a loser, even if the balance sheet can hide the loss by rounding out the numbers. Managers are both listening more carefully to their people and asking them tougher questions. They are looking at their businesses and asking, "How can we create more value?" Answering that question will make companies lean and mean, run faster and be more agile, achieve world-class success—all the words that describe the new world of the business leader.

Unquestionably, globalization is a large part of this new age, not only in terms of products but also in the range of decisions that managers must make. Today a lot of people talk about the global market—but only a very small group understand what it really is. It's not a transnational corporation. It's a horizontal integration of production across many different countries. If you have value added in ten countries, in the end you don't export a product; you export value added. How you integrate that entire operation requires a different set of skills than if you simply set out to build a green-field plant in Spain to make widgets.

Years ago, the economist Milton Friedman called a lot of attention to Leonard Read's story of the simple, old-fashioned lead pencil by using it to illustrate the role of prices in communicating in the marketplace. Today you could use that same lead pencil to illustrate the impact of the globalization of business. In the first place, that old-fashioned lead pencil isn't made out of wood anymore. It's made out of plastic—plastic that looks like wood, has a wood feel, and even sharpens like wood. But it's plastic nonetheless. And the plastic could have been made in a distant foreign country or it could have been made in Detroit or it could have been made in a small town in the South. The carbon for the lead pencil came from still another source and the eraser from a third source. And after it's all been assembled and delivered to the store and it comes time for you to buy that pencil, you don't really care where all the components came from.

That's the globalization of business from the customer's point of view. From the manager's viewpoint, you're in a marketplace where you're suddenly waking up with a guy you've never heard of from a coun-

The whole world is restructuring, driven by the global marketplace.

try you're not too sure where it is, who's eating your lunch in your hometown. That's new. And it requires new skills in managers—it means that leaders must have a wide enough span, a broad enough vision to understand that world and operate in it. It means that they must understand the law of comparative advantage. They need to know that for some production phases, they will not necessarily find comparative advantage in Des Moines, Iowa. It may be in Taiwan or Mexico or some equally good place. They have to be able to decide that, if that's where the value added should be, that's where they'll put it.

Make no mistake—this isn't just a managerial issue for large corporations. In fact, what fascinates me are the little companies that are far ahead in making global decisions. Take, for example, one little $300 million New England-based company that makes connectors. It makes the pins in Switzerland, assembles them in Germany, and sells them here. That would not have been possible 20 years ago.

Of course, it's just as true for the largest corporations. Again, take GE as an example. It makes the high end of its CAT scanners in Milwaukee, Wisconsin—and that equipment is the best in the world. For the low end of the market—a $1 million piece of equipment—it turns to Japan for manufacture. And the middle market in other equipment is covered by General Electric CGR S.A. in Europe. This is a completely global market. Engineering skills pass horizontally from the United States to Japan to France and back again. Each subsidiary company supplies the marketing skills to its own home market.

But the best example is IBM's superconductivity project. It's a global R&D exercise pioneered in Switzerland by the U.S. company working with the talents of a German scientist and a Swiss scientist. Talent doesn't carry a passport in this new age. In fact, to be successful, managers must be able to work with people who don't speak their language, who may not share their value systems, but who have the talent the business needs.

It's true of individuals. But it's also true of other companies from other countries. Because the pretty girl at the party today is named "Alliances." It's named marketing agreements, partnerships, and joint ventures. That's how managers are learning to compete against world-class competitors in a global market. All of this horizontal integration, global production, transborder capital flows, all linked together by an electronic global marketplace—all of this has so locked the world together that politicians worldwide have no choice but to accept it or watch their nation fall behind. The drive toward the European Community 1992 in the Common Market isn't being led by the bureaucrats, the customs clerks, and passport stampers who will all be out of a job. Business is driving it. The Italians were first, largely because many of their businesses had to operate almost in spite of their government. Then came the French, followed now by the Germans, who were slow off the mark. Now it's going on around the world. The New Zealanders are on the hunt—they're looking at alliances and markets. The whole world is restructuring, driven by the realization that it's a global marketplace. Borders and control of land are less and less important. The traditional notion of sovereignty is becoming obsolete. All of this will create immense management problems in the future that will have to be handled with skill—and some alliances will fail.

Globalization is one big change that U.S. managers are now confronting around the world; there are also several important issues here at home that command our attention. We must reconsider many of the systems and assumptions that underlie how we do business and how we manage. Too often we try to apply tools from the Industrial Age to the Information Age. We might as well attempt to power our modern ships with men at oars, all lined up and facing backward, rather than using the latest technology and a forward-looking crew.

Here is just one example: our accounting system. It was designed for a rapidly fading Industrial Age—and it ignores the new realities of the information society. Today FASB is looking at the question of what constitutes an asset. Now, in my book, an asset is something that creates a stream of income. But take that definition and apply it to the modern factory. Today the biggest asset in the business is intellectual capital, the software that actually runs the factory, that controls the operation and makes it productive. But how do we treat software? Because software came after the Industrial Revolution, because it isn't tangible, we expense most of it. And how do we treat the plant – the shell that stands idle until the software brings it to life? We capitalize it. When you know for a fact that if all the software disappeared, all the planes would stop flying, all the streetlights would go off, all the plants would stop producing – and you still can say with a straight face that software isn't an asset – then you must acknowledge an enormous gap between reality and practice.

The same is true in the way we now treat company names. Accounting says that the name Citibank or Coca-Cola or IBM or Apple is valueless; it is "good will." It should be written off – as if 100 years of marketing had no value. But common sense tells you that a trademark is worth something. Otherwise it wouldn't be patentable. And if you look at how some of America's oldest, established companies have tried to put their names back to work for them in the marketplace as a store of value, then it's clear that a company's name can be worth more than its prestigious headquarters building. Especially since some of these companies are fighting to keep their good names and simultaneously selling off their fancy buildings.

The fact is that this system is backward, obsolete. But if you say that out loud, if you try to operate in a way that actually conforms to the way the world now works, then the keepers of the accounting flame accuse you of cooking the books and watering the balance sheet.

There's another accounting problem that's even worse, and that's our national accounts. These numbers are so bad that even the daily newspapers are starting to notice it – but smart managers have known it for years. The problem is this: Washington comes out with GNP numbers that are revised several times and aren't final for three years. And when they're finally adjusted, it often turns out that they're double or half what the government had first announced. It poses a very difficult question for U.S. managers: How do you make decisions in a society where the numbers aren't any good? It is more than ironic that we live in an information-driven economy where

much of the critical information the government puts out is simply inaccurate. And as a consequence, managers must think longer term in all their decisions – but not necessarily for a good reason. Rather, your thinking becomes longer term when you know that all your decisions in the present are based on information that is totally untrustworthy. In that situation, the manager has to rely on his or her instinct and on the passage of time to illuminate what is missing from unreliable statistics.

Another important element of the information society is the change it is bringing in the work force. We are going to continue to see growth in the importance of the knowledge worker compared with the manual worker. It is simply a matter of power and leverage. I remember a presentation on handheld calculators that I attended years ago when they were first appearing. In front of a group of doubting CEOs was a visionary, defending the notion of the calculator, trying to convince these tough-minded managers of its value. Of course, they knew better. "I don't need one of those things," was their attitude. "I know how to add and subtract." And what he told them back then about the simple handheld calculator was this: "You can dig a hole with a shovel too, but it's better to have a bulldozer. What I'm giving you is the hydraulics of the mind." That stopped some of those stiff-collared boys. Because the hydraulics of the mind is what is transforming the entire world. Intellectual capital is becoming relatively more important than physical capital.

We have one more important piece of work to attend to in the United States – and that is education. Our education system and our approach to its problems are perfect reflections of the pluralism of America. And one of our redeeming features is that, if something gets bad enough in this country and if people come to understand it, then we work on that problem. That's the case with education today.

In New York, the most pluralistic of all cities, we probably have the five best schools in the world – and the five worst. The Bronx High School of Science will likely produce more Nobel laure-

Too often we try to apply tools from the Industrial Age to the Information Age.

ates than any school in the world. And it sits in a neighborhood that is a disaster. We have the Manhattan Center for Science and Mathematics, which graduated 100% of its entering class. We have School District 4, which is a model for the world. This district in East Harlem serves over 14,000 students, 60% Hispanic, 35% black, 4% white, 1% Asian. About 80% are eligible for free or reduced-price lunch programs. Its students show dramatic progress compared with students in other districts. And we also know that we have many kids who can't read and write and a huge bureaucracy that shows little interest in change because it's job threatening.

But we know one solution: free choice – creating a marketplace in education. And what's more, we know this isn't the first time we've had to deal with this problem. Years ago, we had people coming right off the boat and into the factory. They couldn't read; they couldn't write. At least not when they started. But we taught them; we taught remedial reading and writing then – today we're teaching remedial computer literacy. It's the same problem.

Is it easy? Of course not. But I believe that we can handle it, that pluralism is our greatest protection. I believe that just as the best land-grant colleges have traditionally challenged the private universities, just as the best public hospitals have challenged private ones – so today in our efforts to improve primary and secondary public education, our greatest strength is choice and pluralism.

Because the most basic fact about the world we live and work in is this: information is a virus that carries freedom. What's happening today in America and around the world is irreversible. While events never move in a straight line without setbacks, what's happening in the Soviet Union, in China, in Eastern Europe is going to change the world. And change it permanently. The Information Age means that there simply isn't anyplace to hide anymore. Whether it's an oil spill in Alaska, a nuclear disaster in Chernobyl, or a massacre in Tiananmen Square, today television shoves that event into more than 100 million homes simultaneously. Information creates freedom because revolutions occur when people become aware of alternatives. And for America and American managers, that's the promise of the best kind of future there is.

Reprint 90116

*At Levi Strauss, the company's most important
asset is its people's "aspirations."*

Values Make the Company:
An Interview with Robert Haas

by Robert Howard

*As chairman and CEO of Levi Strauss & Co., Robert D.
Haas has inherited a dual legacy. Ever since its founding
in 1850, the San Francisco-based apparel manufacturer has been famous for combining strong commercial
success with a commitment to social values and to its
work force.*

*Achieving both goals was relatively easy throughout
much of the postwar era, when the company's main
product – Levi's jeans – became an icon of American pop
culture and sales surged on the demographic wave of the
expanding baby boom. But in the uncertain economic climate of the 1980s, Haas and his management team have
had to rethink every facet of the business – including its
underlying values.*

*Since his appointment as CEO in 1984, Haas has rede-
fined the company's business strategy; created a flatter
organization, including the painful step of cutting the
work force by one-third; and invested heavily in new-
product development, marketing, and technology. In
1985, he and his team took the company private in one
of the most successful management-led LBOs of the
1980s. And in 1987, he oversaw the development of
the Levi Strauss Aspirations Statement, a major initiative to define the shared values that will guide both
management and the work force. (See the insert "Aspirations Statement.")*

*Many CEOs talk about values, but few have gone to the
lengths Haas has to bring them to the very center of how
he runs the business. The Aspirations Statement is shap-
ing how the company defines occupational roles and responsibilities, conducts performance evaluations, trains
new employees, organizes work, and makes business
decisions.*

*The result is a remarkably flexible and innovative
company, despite its age and size. Levi is a pioneer in using electronic networks to link the company more closely
to its suppliers and retailers. The Dockers line of clothing,
introduced in 1986, has been one of the fastest growing
new products in apparel industry history. And the company has made a successful major push into global markets. In 1989, international operations accounted for 34%
of Levi's total sales and 45% of pretax operating profit.*

*Levi's financial results have also been extraordinary.
From 1985 to 1989, sales increased 31% to $3.6 billion.
And profits have risen fivefold to $272 million.*

*Meanwhile, the company has stayed true to its tradi-
tional commitment to social issues even as it has up-
dated that commitment to reflect the economic and
social realities of a new era. Levi Strauss has an exem-
plary record on issues ranging from work force diversity
to benefits for workers dislocated by plant closings and
technological change. Haas himself is the foremost corporate spokesperson on the responsibilities of business in
the AIDS crisis.*

*Reinventing the Levi Strauss heritage has a special
meaning for Haas. He is the great-great-grandnephew of the
company founder, and his uncle, father, and grandfather
all led the company before him. He joined Levi Strauss in
1973 and has served in a variety of leadership positions,
including senior vice president of corporate planning and
policy, president of the operating groups, and executive
vice president and chief operating officer. He has also
worked as an associate at McKinsey & Co. and spent two
years as a Peace Corps volunteer in the Ivory Coast.*

*The interview was conducted at Levi's San Francisco
headquarters by HBR associate editor Robert Howard.*

HBR: *Levi Strauss has long had a reputation for its social responsibility. Why are you placing so much emphasis on defining the company's values now?*

Robert Haas: Levi has always treated people fairly and cared about their welfare. The usual term is "paternalism." But it is more than paternalism, really – a genuine concern for people and a recognition that people make this business successful.

In the past, however, that tradition was viewed as something separate from how we ran the business. We always talked about the "hard stuff" and the "soft

> ## "A company's values – what it stands for, what its people believe in – are crucial to its competitive success."

stuff." The soft stuff was the company's commitment to our work force. And the hard stuff was what really mattered: getting pants out the door.

What we've learned is that the soft stuff and the hard stuff are becoming increasingly intertwined. A company's values – what it stands for, what its people believe in – are crucial to its competitive success. Indeed, values drive the business.

What is happening in your environment to bring you to that conclusion?

Traditionally, the business world had clear boundaries. Geographical or regional borders defined the marketplace. Distinctions between suppliers and customers, workers and managers, were well defined. Once you had a strong market position, you could go on for a long time just on inertia. You could have a traditional, hierarchical, command-and-control organization, because change happened so slowly.

People's expectations for work were also narrowly defined. They gave their loyalty and their efforts in exchange for being taken care of. They expected information and commands to come down from on high, and they did what they were told.

As a result of all the tumult of the 1980s – increased competition, corporate restructurings, the globalization of enterprises, a new generation entering the work force – those traditional boundaries and expectations are breaking down.

What do those changes mean for leadership?

There is an enormous diffusion of power. If companies are going to react quickly to changes in the marketplace, they have to put more and more accountability, authority, and information into the hands of the people who are closest to the products and the customers. That requires new business strategies and different organizational structures. But structure and strategy aren't enough.

This is where values come in. In a more volatile and dynamic business environment, the controls have to be conceptual. They can't be human anymore: Bob Haas telling people what to do. It's the *ideas* of a business that are controlling, not some manager with authority. Values provide a common language for aligning a company's leadership and its people.

Why isn't a sound business strategy enough to create that alignment?

A strategy is no good if people don't fundamentally believe in it. We had a strategy in the late 1970s and early 1980s that emphasized diversification. We acquired companies, created new brands, and applied our traditional brand to different kinds of apparel. Our people did what they were asked to do, but the problem was, they didn't believe in it.

The big change at Levi is that we have worked hard to listen to our suppliers, our customers, and our own people. We have redefined our business strategy to focus on core products, and we have articulated the values that the company stands for – what we call our Aspirations. We've reshaped our business around this strategy and these values, and people have started marching behind this new banner. In fact, they are running to grab it and take it on ahead of senior management. Because it's what they *want* to do.

At Levi, we talk about creating an "empowered" organization. By that, we mean a company where the people who are closest to the product and the customer take the initiative without having to check with anyone. Because in an organization of 31,000 people, there's no way that any one of us in management can be around all the time to tell people what to do. It has to be the strategy and the values that guide them.

What is the role of a manager in an empowered company?

If the people on the front line really are the keys to our success, then the manager's job is to help those people and the people that they serve. That goes against the traditional assumption that the manager is in control. In the past, a manager was expected to know everything that was going on and to be deeply involved in subordinates' activities.

I can speak from experience. It has been difficult for me to accept the fact that I don't have to be the smartest guy on the block—reading every memo and signing off on every decision. In reality, the more

> **"It's the *ideas* of a business that are controlling, not some manager with authority."**

you establish parameters and encourage people to take initiatives within those boundaries, the more you multiply your own effectiveness by the effectiveness of other people.

So in a business world without boundaries, the chief role of managers is to establish some?

To set parameters. Those parameters are going to be different for different individuals. And for the same individual, they're going to be different for different tasks. Some people are going to be very inexperienced in certain things, so you need to be careful about setting the parameters of where they have authority and where they need to stop to seek clarification. Other people have experience, skills, and a track record, and within certain areas you want to give them a lot of latitude.

How does that compare with the traditional manager's job?

In many ways, it's a much tougher role because you can't rely on your title or unquestioning loyalty and obedience to get things done. You have to be thoughtful about what you want. You have to be clear about

---

ASPIRATIONS STATEMENT

We all want a company that our people are proud of and committed to, where all employees have an opportunity to contribute, learn, grow, and advance based on merit, not politics or background. We want our people to feel respected, treated fairly, listened to, and involved. Above all, we want satisfaction from accomplishments and friendships, balanced personal and professional lives, and to have fun in our endeavors.

When we describe the kind of Levi Strauss & Co. we want in the future, what we are talking about is building on the foundation we have inherited: affirming the best of our company's traditions, closing gaps that may exist between principles and practices, and updating some of our values to reflect contemporary circumstances.

What type of leadership is necessary to make our Aspirations a Reality?

New Behaviors: Leadership that exemplifies directness, openness to influence, commitment to the success of others, willingness to acknowledge our own contributions to problems, personal accountability, teamwork, and trust. Not only must we model these behaviors but we must coach others to adopt them.

Diversity: Leadership that values a diverse work force (age, sex, ethnic group, etc.) at all levels of the organization, diversity in experience, and diversity in perspectives. We have committed to taking full advantage of the rich backgrounds and abilities of all our people and to promoting a greater diversity in positions of influence. Differing points of view will be sought; diversity will be valued and honesty rewarded, not suppressed.

Recognition: Leadership that provides greater recognition—both financial and psychic—for individuals and teams that contribute to our success. Recognition must be given to all who contribute: those who create and innovate and also those who continually support the day-to-day business requirements.

Ethical Management Practices: Leadership that epitomizes the stated standards of ethical behavior. We must provide clarity about our expectations and must enforce these standards through the corporation.

Communications: Leadership that is clear about company, unit, and individual goals and performance. People must know what is expected of them and receive timely, honest feedback on their performance and career aspirations.

Empowerment: Leadership that increases the authority and responsibility of those closest to our products and customers. By actively pushing responsibility, trust, and recognition into the organization, we can harness and release the capabilities of all our people.

the standards that you're setting. You have to negotiate goals with your work group rather than just set them yourself. You have to interact personally with individuals whom you're dealing with, understand their strengths and shortcomings, and be clear about what you want them to do.

You also have to accept the fact that decisions or recommendations may be different from what you would do. They could very well be better, but they're going to be different. You have to be willing to take your ego out of it.

That doesn't mean abdication. Managers still have to make decisions, serve as counselors and coaches, be there when things get sticky, and help sort out all the tangles.

What else do managers in an empowered organization need to do?

They can clear away the obstacles to effective action that exist in any large organization. In most companies, including ours, there is a gap between what the organization says it wants and what it feels like to work there. Those gaps between what you say and what you do erode trust in the enterprise and in the leadership, and they inhibit action. The more you can narrow that gap, the more people's energies can be released toward company purposes.

Most people want to make a contribution and be proud of what they do. But organizations typically teach us bad habits—to cut corners, protect our own turf, be political. We've discovered that when people talk about what they want for themselves and for their company, it's very idealistic and deeply emotional. This company tells people that idealism is OK. And the power that releases is just unbelievable. Liberating those forces, getting the impediments out of the way, that's what we as managers are supposed to be doing.

What is happening in the apparel business that makes managing by values so important?

The same things that are happening in most businesses. For decades, apparel has been a very fragmented industry. Most producers were small. Typically, changes in manufacturing technology, the use of computers, and the application of marketing techniques came slowly if at all. Our customers were also highly fragmented. In the old days, we had some 18,000 domestic accounts of all sizes and in every town in the country.

In this environment, we considered ourselves a manufacturer. Our job was to design products, manufacture them, deliver them in accordance with our retailers' orders, and support the retailers with some consumer advertising to help the products sell. But the rest was up to the individual retailer.

Now all that is changing very rapidly. Today the top 50 accounts make up a large part of our domestic business. Style changes happen more rapidly because of innovations in fabric finishes and also because customers adopt new fashions more quickly. Technology is transforming sewing work and our relationships with our suppliers and customers. And we are operating in a global marketplace against international competition. As a result, the way we see our business has also changed.

What's the new vision?

First, we are a marketer rather than a manufacturer. And second, we are at the center of a seamless web of mutual responsibility and collaboration.

Take our relationships with our retailers: to secure the availability of a product, apparel retailers have traditionally had to order it as much as four to five months in advance. That's crazy. It forces retail buyers to guess four and five months down the road what a consumer who is 15 years old is going to want in jeans. During that time, a new movie can come out, and the trend goes from blue denim to black denim. And suddenly that inventory commitment is obsolete, causing costly markdowns.

One answer to this new circumstance is technology. Our electronic data-interchange system, LeviLink, was a pioneering effort in apparel to communicate with our customers and manage the order-replenishment cycle faster and more accurately than conventional systems could. [See the insert "How Values Shape Technology."] As a result, we have customers operating with 20% to 30% less inventory and achieving 20% to 30% increased sales. Their return on their investment with us is much greater than it was in the past. And these retailers also serve their customers better because the desired product is in stock when the consumer goes to purchase it.

We're also forming closer relationships with our suppliers. We used to have ten or twelve U.S. denim suppliers. Now we're down to four or five. There is a seamless partnership, with interrelationships and mutual commitments, straight through the chain that would've been unimaginable ten years ago. You can't be responsive to the end-consumer today unless you can count on those kinds of collaborations at each step along the way.

What are the implications of that seamless partnership for your work force?

Our employees have many new responsibilities. For example, because of our computer linkages to our customers, our account representatives have more information on what's selling at the store level than the retailer does—not only products but sizes, fabrics, and styles. The rep has to know how to analyze that information and interpret it for the customer. What's more, since the computer does all the mundane record-keeping now, the rep can concentrate on planning and projecting the store's needs and being a marketing consultant.

What our employees do for the retailers is also much broader. In addition to the account representative, we have merchandising coordinators who make sure the stock is replenished and train salesclerks so they know how to sell our products more effectively. We have specialists in "visual merchandising" who work with our accounts to improve the ways they display our products. We have promotions experts who help stores tailor promotions to their clientele. And we run consumer hot lines to help customers find the products they want.

The work is much more creative, more entrepreneurial. It's as if these people are in business for themselves. They're doing what human beings do best—think, plan, interact, see trends, humanize the business to make it more successful.

What does that have to do with values?

To do that kind of work effectively requires a whole new set of attitudes and behaviors. The passivity and dependence of traditional paternalism—doing what you're told—doesn't work anymore. People have to take responsibility, exercise initiative, be accountable for their own success and for that of the

How Values Shape Technology

According to Chief Information Officer Bill Eaton, the Levi Strauss & Co. technology strategy is a direct reflection of the company's Aspirations Statement. "Empowerment is meaningless unless people have access to information," says Eaton. "The goal of our technology strategy is to make sure that the information is available on the desktop of the person who is doing the job."

To that end, Levi Strauss has embarked on a three-part program for the global integration of its business through information technology. The most visible part of this strategy is LeviLink, the electronic data-interchange system that ties retailers to the company's distribution network. The system collects point-of-sale information from cash registers at the company's major accounts, then uses the information to generate reorders, invoices, packing slips, and advance notifications to retailers of future shipments. It also provides company sales representatives with far more information on the activity of individual retailers than was available in the past. Currently, about 40% of the company's business comes through LeviLink—a figure that the company hopes to double over the next five years.

Although less visible, Levi Strauss has also made major strides in computerizing its manufacturing operations. In 10 of the company's 32 factories worldwide, every sewing station now comes equipped with a hand-sized computer terminal. As a bundle of fabric moves through the plant, each employee who works on it passes the bundle's bar-coded label through a scanner built into the terminal. The result is a "real-time production control" system that allows the company to track work-in-process as it moves through the factory. The system also provides workers with information on their own performance, which they can use to increase productivity.

The ultimate goal is to link these two systems, allowing the company to issue production orders for new products immediately as existing products are sold in retailers' stores. This capacity will be provided by the Levi's Advanced Business System (LABS), which the company will be implementing over the next three years. LABS will be able to track a product from its conception—including orders, inventory, and financial information. Based on a new "relational database" software architecture, LABS will allow employees to perform more powerful and more flexible searches of company databases and to get rapid access to information typically limited in the past to managers.

The way Levi Strauss manages the development of new systems also reflects its commitment to using technology to support people. CIO Eaton serves on the company's executive management committee, ensuring the integration of technology and business strategies. And close ties between the information systems and human resources departments—one HR staff member now works in information systems—help connect the development of the company's new information technology platform to the creation of new business processes, organization designs, and people skills.

company as a whole. They have to communicate more frequently and more effectively with their colleagues and their customers.

In a traditional command-and-control organization, acting in this way is difficult, even risky. The Aspirations encourage and support the new behaviors that we need. For example, in an empowered organization there are bound to be a lot more disagreements. Because we value open and direct com-

> ## "Because we value open and direct communication, we give people permission to disagree."

munication, we give people permission to disagree. They can tell a manager, "It doesn't seem aspirational to be working with that contractor because from what we've seen, that company really mistreats its workers." Or they can say, "It may help us conserve cash to be slow in paying our bills, but that company has been a supplier for a long time, and it's struggling right now. Wouldn't it be better in terms of the partnership we're trying to create with our suppliers to pay our bills on time?"

Those are very challenging discussions for peers to have—let alone for somebody to have with his or her boss. But if we can "sanctify" it by reference to commonly held standards that we all share, it makes it all right to disagree.

So the values help bring about the kind of business behavior you need to stay competitive.

Values are where the hard stuff and the soft stuff come together. Let me give another example: in the new, more dynamic business environment, a company has to understand the relationship between work and family. It used to be that what happened to your employees when they went home at the end of the day was their business. But today that worker's sick child *is* your business, because if she's worrying about her child or calling in sick when she isn't—and probably feeling resentful because she's had to lie— she isn't going to be productive.

By contrast, if employees aren't worrying about things outside the workplace, if they feel supported—not just financially but "psychically"—then they are going to be more responsive to the needs of customers and of the business. That support needs to come in a whole set of managerial areas: supervisory practices, peer relations, training, work organization, access to information, and the like.

What is Levi doing about this particular issue?

We've established a companywide task force that's looking at how to balance work and family commitments. In itself, that's no big deal. A lot of companies are studying the issue. But even the way we manage the task force reflects our values. For instance, I'm on the task force, but I don't run it. We have everyone from secretaries and sewing machine operators to senior managers on the task force—as part of our commitment to diversity.

And that too makes perfect business sense. After all, my family situation is about as traditional as it gets. I have a wife at home who looks after our daughter. What do I know about the problems of a sewing machine operator—expected to punch in at a certain time and punch out at another and with a half-hour lunch break—whose child's day-care arrangements fall through that morning? Obviously, a better result is going to come out of a broad task force that represents a diversity of opinions, family situations, and points of view. [See the insert "The Making of an Aspiration."]

How does a CEO manage for values?

The first responsibility for me and for my team is to examine critically our own behaviors and manage-

ANDY
WARHOL
LEVI'S
501
JEANS

ment styles in relation to the behaviors and values that we profess and to work to become more consistent with the values that we are articulating. It's tough work. We all fall off the wagon. But you can't be one thing and say another. People have unerring detection systems for fakes, and they won't put up with them. They won't put values into practice if you're not.

You said it's tough. What are the common kinds of breakdowns?

It's difficult to unlearn behaviors that made us successful in the past. Speaking rather than listening. Valuing people like yourself over people of different genders or from different cultures or parts of the organization. Doing things on your own rather than collaborating. Making the decision yourself instead of asking different people for their perspectives. There's a whole range of behaviors that were highly functional in the old hierarchical organization that are dead wrong in the flatter, more responsive, empowered organization that we're seeking to become.

Once your own behavior is in line with the new values, how do you communicate the values to others?

One way is to model the new behaviors we are looking for. For example, senior managers try to be explicit about our vulnerability and failings. We talk to people about the *bad* decisions we've made. It demystifies senior management and removes the stigma traditionally associated with taking risks. We also talk about the limitations of our own knowledge, mostly by inviting other people's perspectives.

> "Senior managers try to be explicit about our vulnerability and failings. We talk to people about the *bad* decisions we've made."

When I talk to employees about the development of the Aspirations Statement, I describe the stark terror I felt when I took over this company, just having turned 43 years old. We were a company in crisis. Our sales were dropping, our international business was heading for a loss, our domestic business had an eroding profit base, our diversification wasn't working, and we had too much production capacity. I had no bold plan of action. I knew that values were important but didn't have the two granite tablets that I

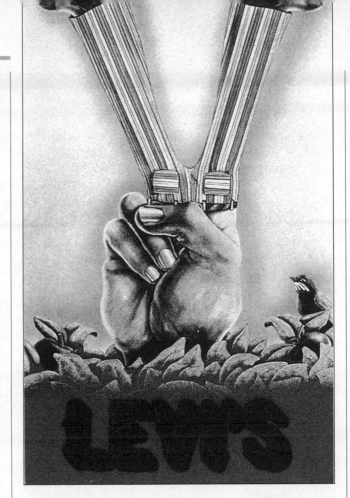

could bring down from Mount Sinai to deliver to the organization. I talk about how alone I felt as a senior manager and how tough it is to be held up as a paragon to the organization. It helps people realize that senior management is human, that we can't be expected to know everything, and that we're inviting them in as partners in the organization.

Another important way to communicate values is through training. We've developed a comprehensive training program that we call the core curriculum. The centerpiece is a week-long course known as "leadership week" that helps managers practice the behavior outlined in the Aspirations Statement. We run about 20 sessions a year for a small group of about 20 people at a time. By the end of this year, the top 700 people in the company will have been through it. And at least one member of the executive management committee—the top 8 people in the company—or some other senior manager participates in every week-long session, just to send a signal of how important this is to us.

Can you really train people in new values?

You can't train anybody to do anything that he or she doesn't fundamentally believe in. That's why we've designed leadership week to give people an opportunity to reflect on their own values and to allow

The Making of an Aspiration

In 1985, a small group of minority and women managers asked for a private meeting with Levi Strauss & Co. CEO Robert Haas. The company had always been committed to equal employment opportunity; compared with other corporations, its numbers were good. But the managers felt strongly that they had reached a plateau. There were invisible barriers keeping women and minorities from advancing in the organization.

In response to their concerns, Haas organized an off-site retreat. Ten senior managers, all white men, were paired with either a woman or minority manager from their work group. The senior managers believed the company had been doing a good job hiring and promoting women and minorities. They were surprised to discover the depth of frustration and anger their subordinates felt. After two-and-a-half days of often painful discussion, the group concluded that equal employment opportunity was not just a matter of numbers but of attitudes, and that considerable unconscious discrimination still existed at the company. Something more needed to be done.

Since that 1985 meeting, Levi Strauss has renewed its commitment to full diversity at all levels. It has also broadened the definition of diversity beyond equal employment opportunity to the active encouragement of different points of view and their inclusion in company decision making.

Between 1985 and 1988, 16 more off-site sessions paired white, male managers with women or minorities who work for them to reflect on unexamined assumptions about diversity and stereotypes about particular groups. In 1987, diversity became one of the six Aspirations defined in the company's Aspirations Statement. That same year, members of the company's executive management committee – the top 8 people in the company – began holding monthly forums for small groups of 15 to 20 employees. By 1989, 20 ongoing forums were taking place. And while the original focus of the meetings was on questions of race and gender, the forums have expanded to consider a broad range of workplace issues.

The forums have been the catalyst for a number of new initiatives:

☐ Recognizing that women and minority employees often have special problems and needs, the company has inaugurated four new career-development courses – one each for women, blacks, Hispanics, and Asians.

☐ These courses have led to the creation of ethnic support networks for blacks, Asians, and Hispanics. Representatives of these networks have direct feedback to top management through quarterly meetings with the senior personnel committee.

☐ In 1989, Levi Strauss established a companywide task force to recommend new policies to support a more effective balance between work and family life. Its 18 members are drawn from all levels of management and the work force – from sewing operators and secretaries to a division president and the CEO. This past summer, the task force sent a 25-page questionnaire to 15,000 of Levi's 21,000 U.S. employees to survey their family needs.

☐ In 1989, the company also inaugurated a three-day course on "Valuing Diversity." About 240 top managers will have taken the course by the end of 1990. Eventually, all Levi Strauss employees will take diversity training.

---

them to say what they want to get from work. In most cases, people learn that their personal values are aligned with those of the company. Of course, not everybody will buy into it. We've had some very honest discussions where managers say, "Look, I'm 53 years old, I've managed one way all my life and been successful, and now the company wants me to change. I don't know if I can do it."

But two things happen during leadership week. Because the groups are small, people build up a support network. They realize that others have the same problems that they have. Suddenly, they don't feel so alone.

Second, the training makes clear what's expected of them and what the consequences of succeeding or failing to adapt will be. It gives people the freedom to opt out. The real success of our core curriculum will be if it convinces some people that our environment is simply not right for them.

We also try to make sure that the core curriculum isn't just some nice experience that stops as soon as people get back to their jobs. For instance, there is a section of leadership week called "unanswered questions" where people voice concerns inspired by the course. Our human resources people collect these unanswered questions and report on them every quarter to the executive management committee. Sometimes, these questions can be handled by a particular individual. In other cases, we've set up a companywide task force to study the issue and come back with suggestions for changes in the way we do things. This creates a dialogue within the company among the people who have to make things happen.

Do the company's values influence the way you evaluate managers?

One-third of a manager's raise, bonus, and other financial rewards depends on his or her ability to manage aspirationally—the "how" of management rather than the "what." That goes for decisions about succession planning as well.

In some areas of the company, they're weighting it even more strongly. The point is, it's big enough to get people's attention. It's real. There's money attached to it. Giving people tough feedback and a low rating on aspirational management means improvement is necessary no matter how many pants they got out the door. Promotion is not in the future unless you improve.

How important is pay for pushing the company's values through the organization?

It's an influence but not the most important one. The key factors determining whether the values take or not will be individual commitment and desire and the peer pressure in the environment that we create. To me, the idea of a person as a marionette whose arms and legs start moving whenever you pull the pay string is too simplistic a notion of what motivates people in organizations.

That goes against the trend in recent years to fine-tune compensation incentives and tie them more closely to performance.

What happens there is you end up using pay to manage your company. But pay shouldn't manage your company; managers should. Managers should set the example, create the expectations, and provide the feedback. Managers should create an environment where people want to move in a constructive direction—not because there's money tied to the end of it, but because they feel it's right and they want to do it. That's why the way we conduct performance evaluations is probably more important than the pay we attach to aspirational management.

What's the process?

The typical performance evaluation in business has a manager set goals for a subordinate at the start of the year, and then at the end of the year make a subjective judgment about how well he or she has fulfilled them. That tends to create rabid "upward serving" behavior. People play to the person who's buttering their bread.

But what constitutes effective performance for a manager, anyway? Not necessarily pleasing your boss. Rather, good managers mobilize the talents of subordinates, peers, and clients to further the group's goals.

So what I started doing years ago—long before we developed the Aspirations Statement—was to talk with the direct reports of the people I manage, as well as with their peers and others they interact with. To evaluate one individual, I might interview anywhere from 10 to 16 people. The discussions are anonymous and confidential. And I report only trends, not isolated incidences.

This is an extremely powerful process that promotes ongoing feedback. The quotes may be anonymous, but they are very direct. "Here's what a group of people who work for you feel: You're much too controlling. You don't give them the latitude they need to show you how much they could do. People feel scared to take risks with you or to say controversial things because you act like you don't believe them."

I also ask the people who contribute to somebody's evaluation to say the same things to the person's face. If we can encourage regular dialogue among people so that they give their bosses or peers feedback on their

performance, managers begin to realize that they have to pay attention to their people. If they create an

> ## "Suddenly, this $4 billion company feels like an owner-operated company, which is the goal."

unwholesome, unproductive environment and can't change it, we're not going to tolerate it.

Has the Aspirations Statement had any impact yet on the quality of major business decisions?

I'm the first to say our journey is incomplete. But compared with, say, five years ago, there definitely is a change. Suddenly, this $4 billion company feels like an owner-operated company, which is the goal.

Take the example of our Dockers product line. Dockers was like a new invention—a brand new segment in the casual pants market. The concept started in Argentina. Our Japanese affiliate picked it up under another name. Our menswear division adapted the idea to the U.S. market under the name of Dockers. Then the other domestic divisions saw its potential, and now it's in womenswear and kidswear. We also have a Shirts Dockers line and in selected international markets, we're seeing the startup of a Dockers product. In 1986, we sold 35,000 units. This year, we'll be doing a half-a-billion-dollar business in the United States.

We didn't have a business plan for Dockers. We had managers who saw an opportunity. They created a product and went out and made commitments for production that were greater than the orders they had in hand, because they believed in the product and its momentum. They got corporate support for an investment in advertising that was not justified on a cost-per-unit basis and created a product that anybody else in the market could have done. And five years later, it's a staple in the American wardrobe. None of this would have happened before this more collaborative, open style of management.

We've talked about getting managers to accept and live the company's values. But more than 75% of Levi's work force consists of operators in your sewing and finishing plants. Isn't the real challenge to make the company's values meaningful for them?

Empowerment isn't limited to just white-collar workers. By utilizing our people more fully than the apparel industry traditionally has, we can organize sewing work in ways that are much more in keeping with our Aspirations. About a year ago, we initiated an experiment at our Blue Ridge, Georgia plant, where we set up a gain-sharing program. We said to the employees, "You are the experts. If you meet predetermined production goals and predetermined absenteeism and safety standards, we'll split 50-50 with you any savings that result from economies or productivity improvements."

Sewing machine operators are now running the plant. They're making the rules and in some cases changing them because they understand why the rules are there and which rules make sense and which don't. They're taking initiatives and making things work better because it's in their interest and they don't have to be told.

This was not an unproductive plant. It was among the top 10% in the company. Today it's one of the top two plants—after only nine months in the new program. The financial payoff has been considerable, and there's certainly more potential there. But to me, the most exciting thing is to see the transformation in the workplace. People who felt that they weren't valued despite maybe 20 years of work for the company have a completely different attitude about their work.

In my judgment, we can restructure the workplace far beyond what we've done in Blue Ridge. I see us moving to a team-oriented, multiskilled environment in which the team itself takes on many of the supervisor's and trainer's tasks. If you combine that with some form of gain sharing, you probably will have a much more productive plant with higher employee satisfaction and commitment.

> ## "You can't promise employment security and be honest. The best you can do is not play games with people."

During the same period in which Levi has been defining its values, you've also been downsizing the company. Is it possible to get a high-commitment work force without offering some kind of employment security?

You can't promise employment security and be honest. The best you can do is not play games with people. You can't make any guarantees.

Through the 1950s, 1960s, and 1970s, Levi was growing so dramatically that unless you committed a felony, you weren't going to lose your job. But that

was a special era stimulated by economic expansion and tremendous demographic growth. Now we're in a real-world situation where market forces are less favorable, external competitive pressures are more intense, and change is more rapid. You have to help people appreciate the need to deal constructively with the changing environment. If we're doing our job, we need to understand the rapidity and magnitude of the changes taking place and provide people with all the tools we can to cope with change.

But isn't it disingenuous to be championing values like empowerment in an environment where workers are worried about losing their jobs?

There is an apparent contradiction but not a real one, because our most basic value is honesty. If we have too much capacity, it's a problem that affects the entire company. Sometimes, the only solution is to close a plant, and if we don't have the guts to face that decision, then we risk hurting a lot of people—not just those in one plant. We need to be honest about that.

We tie it to Aspirations by asking, "How are we going to treat people who are displaced by technology, by changes in production sources, or by market changes?" We are committed to making the transition as successful as possible and to minimizing the uprooting and dislocation. We give more advance notice than is required by law. We provide more severance than is typical in our industry, so the effect of displacement is cushioned. We extend health care benefits. We also support job-training programs and other local initiatives to help our former employees find new jobs. And in the community itself, which has been depending on us as a major employer, we continue for a period of time to fund community organizations and social causes that we've been involved with, so that our withdrawal isn't a double hit—a loss of employment and also a loss of philanthropic support.

But has the Aspirations Statement changed the way you make decisions about capacity and plant closings in the first place?

The Aspirations make us slow down decisions. We challenge ourselves more explicitly to give some factors more weight than we did before—especially the impact of a plant closing on the community. There have been plants we have decided not to close, even though their costs were higher than other plants we did close. The reason was the community impact.

The Aspirations also provide a way to talk about these difficult trade-offs inside the company. People now have the freedom and authority to say, "Is it aspirational to be closing a plant when we're having a good year?" Or, "If we must close this plant, are we meeting our responsibilities to the employees and their community?" That forces us to be explicit about all the factors involved. It causes us to slow up, reflect, and be direct with one another about what's happening.

If the company's values cause you to slow up, doesn't that make it more difficult to respond to fast-changing markets?

Only if you assume it's still possible to separate the hard stuff from the soft stuff. Most managers say they want to optimize their business decisions. My personal philosophy is to suboptimize business decisions. Too often, optimizing really means taking only one dimension of a problem into account. Suboptimizing means looking at more than one factor and taking into account the interests and the needs of all the constituents. When you do that, suddenly the traditional hard values of business success and the nontraditional soft values relating to people start blending. The result is a better business decision—and it can still be done quickly if your employees understand the company's values and are empowered to take action without layers of review.

You mentioned collecting "unanswered questions" from employees about the role of values in the business. What's the most difficult for you to answer?

One of the most frequent things I hear is: "When the next downturn in the business happens, is top management going to remain committed to Aspirations?" The only answer to that one is, "Test us." We hope we won't have a downturn, but even if we do, I have no doubts about what management's commitment is. Only the experience of going through that kind of a situation, however, will convincingly demonstrate that commitment.

Where is that commitment to let values drive the business leading?

We've launched an irreversible process. Now we have to support the commitment that the Aspirations Statement is creating and be willing to deal with the tough issues that it raises.

Two years ago, I gave a speech about the Aspirations at one of our worldwide management meetings. At the end, I held up the Aspirations Statement and ripped it to shreds. And I said, "I want each of you to throw away the Aspirations Statement and think about what you want for the company and what kind of person you want to be in the workplace and what kind of a legacy you want to leave behind. If the result happens to be the Aspirations, that's fine. But if it happens to be something else, the important thing is that you think deeply about who you are and what you stand for. I have enough confidence in your judgment and motivations that I'll go with whatever you come up with."

The point is, the Levi Strauss of the future is not going to be shaped by me or even by the Aspirations Statement. It's going to be shaped by our people and their actions, by the questions they ask and the responses we give, and by how this feeds into the way we run our business. ⬨

Reprint 90504

The new industrial competition

The results of Japanese competition in U.S. markets are evident to all Americans. Repercussions from competitive pressures exerted by European and Japanese manufacturers have been or are being felt by U.S. producers of cars, machine tools, minicomputers, commercial aircraft, textile machinery, and color TV sets, to name a few traditional businesses. Taking auto manufacture as their case example, the authors of this article attribute the Japanese carmakers' success to superiority in the manufacturing plant, especially in their process systems and work force management.

The authors describe the current dilemma of U.S. car manufacturers, who find themselves at a crossroads because this struggle has changed the rules of the game. Now these producers face a situation in which advancing technology and the momentous changes it wreaks—instead of the incremental changes through styling, marketing, and service to which U.S. manufacturers are accustomed—will determine the winners and losers. As often happens in a mature industry when a new phase of competition appears, the auto industry may well undergo a renewal that transforms it. The challenge for U.S. companies in endangered industries is to recognize the altered situation, adjust to it, and learn to manage change.

Thrown into a competitive turmoil, a mature industry can go through a rejuvenation— as U.S. auto manufacturing appears ready to do

William J. Abernathy,
Kim B. Clark, and
Alan M. Kantrow

William Abernathy is professor of business administration at the Harvard Business School. A noted expert on the automobile industry, he wrote The Productivity Dilemma: Roadblock to Innovation in the Automobile Industry (Johns Hopkins University Press, 1978). Kim Clark, assistant professor of business administration at the Harvard Business School, is author of the National Academy of Sciences' forthcoming report on The Competitive Status of the U.S. Automobile Industry. Alan Kantrow, an associate editor at HBR, has written two previous HBR articles, the more recent being "The Strategy-Technology Connection" (July-August 1980.)

Reprint 81501

It is barely possible that in some remote corner of the United States a latter-day Rip Van Winkle awoke this morning fresh with shining images of American industry in the 1950s still fixed in his head. But it is not very likely. Who, after all, during the past few years could have slept undisturbed through the general chorus of lament about the economy? Who could have remained unaware that much of U.S. industry—especially the mature manufacturing sector—has fallen on hard times?

And who did not have a surefire remedy? Born-again supply-siders argued for the massive formation of capital; "new class" advocates of a more systematic industrial policy, for better allocation of existing capital; industrial economists, for enhanced productivity; organized labor, for a coherent effort at reindustrialization; subdued (if unrepentant) Keynesians, for more artful demand management; boisterous Lafferites, for a massive tax cut; congressional experts, for carefully targeted tax breaks on depreciation and investment; Friedmanites, for tight money; and Naderites, for an anticorporate economic democracy.

This loudly divided counsel on the best strategy for managing economic change reflects inadequacy in both perception and understanding: our current industrial malaise defies the usual interpretations and resists the usual prescriptions. Managing change successfully has proved difficult because policymakers in business and government, trained in an old economic calculus, have found it hard to see the new competitive realities for what they are—or to identify the best terms in which to analyze them.

Policymakers fail to understand that the old rules of thumb and worn assumptions no longer hold. Similarly, the traditional structural arrangements in many industries—the familiar relationship between, say, labor and management or producer and supplier—no longer square with the facts of competitive life. As a result, decision makers who continue to act as if nothing has happened are, at best, ineffective and, at worst, inadvertent agents of economic disaster.

Levers of change

What has happened? The two principal changes have been greater exposure to international competition and technical advances that alter competition. For a start, let's look at two basic major manufacturing industries that have experienced these forces.

One is color television:

☐ This industry was confronted with new competitors who emphasized high productivity, reliability, quality, and competent design (but not innovative design, except for Sony).

☐ Many competitors—Warwick, Motorola, and Admiral among them—did not survive the foreign thrust and were either taken over or went out of business.

☐ Foreign competitors' emphasis on manufacturing, a critical element, was transferred to their U.S. operations—witness Sanyo's management of the previously unsuccessful old Warwick plant, with many of the same employees and U.S. middle managers.

☐ Now technological changes have created a situation of potential renewal of the product life cycle—developments in videocassette recorders; videodiscs; flat, high-resolution screens; telecommunications; and computers may combine to revolutionize the television business.

. . . And another is textile machinery:

☐ Before the 1960s a few U.S. manufacturers (for example, Draper) dominated this business. Conglomerates acquired them (e.g., Rockwell International took over Draper).

☐ The U.S. manufacturers began to lose business primarily because of deterioration in product performance relative to European and Japanese models and failure to remain at the cutting edge of new technology.

☐ Because of insufficient investment (conglomerates treated them as cash cows), the once-dominant U.S. manufacturers have lost technical and market leadership to the Swiss, Germans, and Japanese.

Now consider two other industries that are facing the new forces of international competition.

One of them is computers:

☐ Fujitsu has introduced a mainframe computer that attacks IBM where its strength is—service. Fujitsu is doing this by building a high-quality, reliable machine that can *guarantee* 99% uptime. In a test run of strategy, Fujitsu has taken on IBM in Australia with this approach and bested the U.S. giant in obtaining some mainframe contracts. The experience there to date: 99.8% uptime.

☐ In minicomputers and home computers the Japanese are entering the U.S. market. Producers like Mitsubishi, Nippon Electric, and Hitachi will soon offer high-quality products that are cost competitive.

. . . And another is machine tools:

☐ Japanese producers have entered this market with a strategy built around a very reliable, high-quality product. Recently, for instance, a U.S. auto producer ordered transfer lines from an established U.S. machine tool manufacturer and from Toyota. The lines arrived at the U.S. plant at the same time. Toyota sent two engineers who had the equipment running and fully debugged in two weeks, while the competitor's team of eight engineers spent several months getting its line operational.

☐ Developments in new technology—electronics, optical and tactile sensors, lasers, and robotics—are creating opportunities for improved metalworking operations and are opening up new applications in areas like assembly and inspection, where mechanization and automation have hardly played a role. Integration of these advances with computerized design and manufacturing could change the very concepts on which traditional machine tools are founded.

A number of other long-stable U.S. manufacturing industries no doubt will be shaken in the not-distant future by these pressures. One is the air compressor field, which a few companies have dominated. A Japanese producer, Hokuetsu, entered its domestic market five years ago and now rules it. Among the companies left in its wake is Ingersoll-Rand, whose market share in Japan plunged from well over 50% to zero. Hokuetsu offers a dependable, good-quality product at half the cost of the comparable U.S. compressor.

Still another field is major household appliances, which the Japanese have slated for heavy export activity in this decade. Sanyo, Toshiba, and other companies are setting up U.S. plants and distribution systems. General Electric, for one, is worried; GE has begun a program designed to improve greatly the quality and productivity of its Louisville appliance complex.

The list of endangered industries goes on: jet engines, commercial aircraft, small forklift trucks, steel, electric motors, lawnmowers, and chainsaws, to name just a few.

Character of the new competition

Let us focus on a single industry to show in detail the character of the conditions that the imperiled U.S. industries face. An inkling of these conditions has entered the consciousness of all Americans as they witnessed Japan's extraordinary success in capturing a large share of the automobile market from the entrenched Big Three domestic producers. In this article we go beyond the previously known facts and show exactly how the Japanese implemented their strategy on the plant floor, on the engineers' design boards, and in the executive offices.

Until recently, developments in the U.S. auto industry were determined mostly by government policies and economic forces peculiar to North America. The sheer extent of the U.S. market and its productive base had long guaranteed the industry a largely self-contained posture. Over the past 15 years, however, the competitive boundaries have expanded drastically until now they are virtually worldwide in scope.

Accompanying this expansion has been a rapid increase in the number of healthy competitors. These new international players, moreover, have quite a different approach from that of the U.S. Big Three; their plan consists of radically new strategies, modes of operation, and production experience.

More to the point, the novel competitive challenge they present cannot be overcome by the familiar responses U.S. companies have long used against each other. Strategically, the Big Three are well prepared to fight not this new war, but the last one.

Many observers believe that the perceived low quality of Detroit's vehicles is a simple function of lethargy and past practice. This view ignores the close connection between poor quality and a disadvantage in costs. The productive capacity of some new entrants, notably the Japanese, enjoys a significant cost advantage over that of the Americans. The Japanese have been especially skillful in exploiting this advantage by adding performance and quality to their cars. This combination of competitive price and high quality has proved tremendously successful in reaching consumers in the American market.

What makes this advantage particularly troublesome is that it does not represent primarily an investment problem; if it did, it would be far easier to remedy. Instead, it arises to some extent from differences in wage rates and, more significant, from differences in productivity and management of operations.

In 1973, when Lee A. Iacocca was asked about the competitive advantage of innovation as perceived by Ford, he responded simply, "Give them [American consumers] leather. They can smell it." In Ford's reading of the U.S. market,

innovation did not pay; styling did. Things are quite different today: technology matters.

In the 1950s and 1960s, product technology was competitively neutral. No auto company sought a competitive advantage through significant innovation. In the 1980s, however, the necessity for advantage through innovation is steadily growing. In fact, consumer preference for small, fuel-efficient automobiles has developed faster in the United States than it did earlier in Europe or Japan. Beset by unfortunate decisions in the past, the continued absence of a workable long-term energy policy, conflicting regulatory requirements, and the massive financial demands posed by a retooling of production capacity, U.S. producers find themselves at a serious technological disadvantage.

But this is not all. The edge that U.S. companies have long enjoyed in mass production technology and in the resulting economies of scale —an edge long believed essential to competitive success—no longer obtains. Most of the standard U.S. technology is either already widely diffused or easily transferable. Moreover, the process technology for the new, smaller autos is subtly but significantly different from that now in place. In other words, changing market preferences and changing rates of technology diffusion have diluted, perhaps destroyed, the established scale economies of U.S. producers.

Premium on management

Two main distinctions have largely provided the structure for discussions of manufacturing competitiveness. The first is the division between analysis and prescription of a "macro" sort (that is, having to do with such overarching questions of economic management as fiscal and monetary policy and tax incentives) and those of a "micro" sort (that is, having to do with issues relating to the management of particular companies). The second is the division between analysis and prescription based on "hardware" (equipment, buildings, and machinery) and those based on "software" (people management, organizational systems, and corporate strategies).

Considered together, these distinctions form the simple matrix shown in *Exhibit I*. Although the distinctions among these quadrants are rough, they are nonetheless useful. In practice, however, they are often neglected, which has left the unfortunate impression in some minds that the current industrial difficulties are composed equally —and indistinguishably—of problems in all the quadrants.

Exhibit I **Key elements in manufacturing competitiveness**

	Macro	Micro
Hardware	1. Government fiscal and monetary policies Taxation Capital markets Savings	2. Production capability Plant Equipment
Software	3. Socioeconomic environment Work ethic Regulation Education	4. Corporate management Organization Administration Production systems

This impression has been mischievous, for these difficulties and their remedies are distributed unevenly about the matrix. In the auto industry the key measures for meeting the new competition fall primarily into Quadrant 4.

Japanese micromanagement

The Japanese advantage in production costs and product quality in the auto industry, as well as many other established U.S. industries, is not only a fact defining the new competitive reality but also the result of a carefully honed approach to management—the stuff of Quadrant 4. Americans' talk of overregulation, underdepreciation, pervasive national culture, and markedly absent government support is misplaced.

Costs of production

Several estimates have placed the landed cost advantage in U.S. markets of Japanese-produced subcompact cars in the $400 to $600 range per vehicle. For example, Abraham Katz, then assistant secretary of commerce for international economic policy, testified last year that "the apparent cost advantage to Japanese producers may have been $560 per car in 1979."[1]

These estimates, in our view, seriously understate the advantage. In the first place, they fail to reflect both current rates of labor compensation and, perhaps more important, the great differences in productivity between Japanese and American manufacturers. Furthermore, they are often based on a narrow definition of the productive units to be compared, for they assume that the relevant comparison is between two original equipment manufacturers—say, Ford and Toyota—even though the really meaningful comparison lies between two productive systems, or "confederations"—that is, an OEM and its constellation of suppliers.

To get a truer picture of the Japanese cost advantage, we must therefore produce estimates that account for productivity differentials, labor costs, and industry structure.

The first step in developing these improved estimates is to update assessments of differential labor productivity. We know that in 1974 output per labor hour in the Japanese auto industry—OEMs and suppliers—was 88% of the level in the United States (that is, the ratio of Japanese to U.S. productivity was 0.88). Published data suggest that growth in labor productivity in the Japanese auto industry (motor vehicles and parts) averaged 8% to 9% in the 1970s; the comparable figure for the United States was 3% to 4%. Using a midrange estimate of the difference (5%), we arrive at a 1980 productivity ratio of 1.18. This means that in 1980 Japanese producers operated at a productivity level almost 20% above that of their American competitors.

This rapid growth was offset in part by higher rates of wage increase: in 1974 Japanese hourly compensation rates were about 37% of those in the United States, while in 1980 they were roughly 50%. Dividing the compensation ratio (0.5) by the productivity ratio (1.18) yields a unit labor cost ratio of 0.424—a figure that has remained more or less constant during the entire 1974-1980 period.

Table A in the *Appendix* translates this steady labor cost ratio into a Japanese advantage of $1,673. Subtracting $400 for freight and tariff costs yields a landed cost advantage of $1,273 on a 1980 subcompact that sells in the American market for about $5,500—a cost advantage of 23%.

Although the calculations in *Table A* are based on a number of undocumented assumptions about cost structure and labor content, reasonable adjustment of these assumptions would not affect the order of magnitude of the Japanese cost advantage. Indeed, we were biased conservatively throughout in estimating that cost advantage. Moreover, inclusion of general administrative and selling expenses, as well as the costs of capital and salaried personnel, would leave the Japanese cost advantage intact. So we figure that Japanese producers enjoy a $1,200 landed cost advantage on every small vehicle sold in the United States.

We can to some extent check these numbers against information in the annual reports of major U.S. and Japanese producers. These reports yield data on the costs of nonlabor inputs and salaried personnel but none on the labor embodied in components or materials.

Getting at these data, however, presents several analytic problems. Perhaps the most serious is the great difference between U.S. and Japanese OEMs in their degree of vertical integration and in the nature of their relationships with suppliers. At Toyota, for example, purchases account for almost 80% of the value of sales; but because Toyota holds an equity interest in many of its suppliers, this figure is somewhat misleading. Comparable data for U.S. companies show much less reliance on suppliers; GM, for instance, has a purchase-to-sale ratio of less than 50%.

A second problem is the quite different product mix of U.S. and Japanese OEMs. The data we use come from 1979, when medium-size cars dominated the U.S. Big Three's product lines. The Japanese were producing a much narrower range of vehicles and, of course, were emphasizing the subcompact segment.

Table B in the *Appendix* shows estimates of total employee costs per vehicle in 1979 at Ford and Toyo Kogyo (Mazda). Our calculations suggest that assembly of the average Ford vehicle required 112.5 employee hours; a Toyo Kogyo vehicle, only 47. Employee costs in building the Ford vehicle were $2,464; for Toyo Kogyo, $491.

As already noted, this sizable cost gap reflects differences in product mix and vertical integration as well as in labor costs and productivity. Information on value added in the annual reports and discussions with industry sources suggest that the Toyo Kogyo results should be increased by 15% to 20% to adjust for vertical integration. Using these higher estimates yields a per-vehicle total of 56 hours instead of 47. (To correct for product mix, we have estimated the cost to Ford of producing the Toyo Kogyo product mix. These calculations are presented in *Table C* in the *Appendix.*)

Our analysis of annual report data suggests that in 1979 the difference between Ford and Toyo Kogyo employee costs per small vehicle was about $1,300. Updating this figure to 1980 might increase the absolute dollar amount somewhat, but the evidence we cited on relative growth rates in productivity and compensation implies that the percentage gap would not change much.

Adjustment for changes in exchange rates would also have a negligible effect. Using a rate of 200 yen to the dollar (the approximate rate at the end of 1980) instead of 218 would reduce the gap by only $50. And when we adjust this $1,300 to reflect the U.S. advantage in administrative and selling expenses, the 2.9% tariff with the relevant freight costs for Japanese imports, and the Japanese productivity edge at the supplier level, we emerge with a landed cost advantage for Japanese OEMs of about $1,400.

Contrasts in product quality

It is, of course, true that the competitively important dimensions of auto quality are established not by experts but by the market. And many American consumers, who place a high value on quality of assembly workmanship (what the industry calls "fits and finishes"), on reliability, and on durability, seem to believe that Japanese cars are superior in each of these dimensions.

Exhibit II, which presents industry data on assembly quality, suggests that consumer perceptions are consistent with experience. Buyers rated the imports as a group superior in quality to the domestically produced cars, while the top Japanese models were ranked first and third among the nine rated. Japanese makes also had fewer defects after one month of service.

Similarly, subscribers to *Consumer Reports* gave high ratings to Japanese autos for reliability as measured by the incidence of repairs (see *Exhibit III*). Nevertheless, what little evidence exists indicates that U.S.-built vehicles have superior corrosion protection and longer-lived components and systems.

At any rate, American automobiles enjoy much less customer loyalty than do Japanese imports. *Exhibit IV*, which summarizes the data on loyalty, gives perhaps the clearest evidence of the differential customer perception of product value for each dollar spent.

Lessons of Quadrant 4

Most explanations of this Japanese advantage in production costs and product quality emphasize the impact of automation, the strong

1. Statement before the Subcommittee on Trade of the House Ways and Means Committee, March 18, 1980.

Exhibit II	Evidence on assembly quality of U.S. autos vs. certain imports		
	Vehicle category	Condition at delivery scale of 1-10; 10 is excellent	Condition after one month of service number of defects per vehicle shipped
	Aggregates	**Domestic**	**Imports**
	Subcompact	6.4	7.9
	Compact	6.2	7.7
	Midsize	6.6	8.1
	Standard	6.8	–
Models	**Domestic**		
	Omni	7.4	4.10
	Chevette	7.2	3.00
	Pinto	6.5	3.70
	Rabbit (U.S.)*	7.8	2.13
	Horizon	7.5	NA
	Imports		
	Civic	8.0	1.23†
	Fiesta	7.9	NA
	Colt	7.8	NA
	Corolla	7.8	0.71‡

*European Rabbit averages 1.42 defects per vehicle shipped.

†Honda average.

‡Toyota average.

Source:
Aggregates – Rogers National Research, *Buyer Profiles*, 1979; models – industry sources.

support of the central government, and the pervasive influence of national culture. No doubt these factors have played an important role, but the primary sources of this advantage are found instead in the Japanese producers' mastery of Quadrant 4—that is, in their execution of a well-designed strategy based on the shrewd use of manufacturing excellence.

It may seem odd to think of manufacturing as anything other than a competitive weapon, yet the history of the U.S. auto market shows that by the late 1950s manufacturing had become a competitively neutral factor. It was not, of course, unimportant, but none of the major American producers sought great advantage through superior manufacturing performance. Except perhaps for their reliance on economies of scale, they tended to compete by means of styling, marketing, and dealership networks.

The Japanese cost and quality advantage, however, originates in painstaking strategic management of people, materials, and equipment—that is, in superior manufacturing performance. This approach, in our view, arose from the Japanese pattern of domestic competition and the need for an effective strategy to enter the U.S. market.

At that time the Japanese realized it would be foolish to compete head-on with the established domestic producers' competence in making elaborately (and annually) styled large cars with a "boulevard ride." They lacked the experience, the manufacturing base, and the resources. Instead, taking a lesson from Volkswagen's success, the Japanese concentrated on producing a reliable, high-quality, solid-performance small automobile and on backing it up with a responsible network of dealers.

Exhibit V outlines the seven factors most responsible for successful productivity performance and compares the Japanese practice in each with the American. On the basis of extensive discussions with U.S. industry executives, engineers, and consultants, we have ranked these factors in the order of their importance in determining the current state of the industry and have given them approximate relative weights.

Surprisingly, the hardware associated with technology—new automation and product design—proves relatively insignificant in assessing the competitive difficulties of the U.S. manufacturers, although its importance for the future of the industry grows ever larger. Despite the publicity given Japan's experimentation with industrial robots and advanced assembly plants like Nissan's Zama facility, the evidence suggests that U.S. producers have so far maintained roughly comparable levels of process equipment. However appealing they may be, Quadrant 2 explanations cannot themselves account for U.S.-Japanese differentials in manufacturing productivity.

Focus on 'process yield'

To the contrary, a valid explanation must start with the factor of "process yield," an amalgam of management practices and systems connected with production planning and control. This yield category reflects Japanese superiority in operating processes at high levels of efficiency and output over long periods of time. Although certain engineering considerations (machine cycles, plant layouts, and the like) are significant here, the Japanese advantage has far more to do with the interaction of materials control systems, maintenance practices, and employee involvement. *Exhibit VI* attempts to make this interaction clear.

At the heart of the Japanese manufacturing system is the concept of "just in time" production. Often called *Kanban* (after the cards or tickets used to trigger production), the system is designed so that materials, parts, and components are produced or delivered just before they are needed. Tight coupling of the manufacturing stages reduces the need for work-in-process inventory. This reduction helps expose any waste of time or materials, use of defective parts, or improper operation of equipment.[2]

Furthermore, because the system will not work if frequent or lengthy breakdowns occur, it creates inescapable pressure for maximizing uptime and minimizing defects. This pressure, in turn, supports a vigorous maintenance program. Most Japanese plants operate with only two shifts, which allows for thorough servicing of equipment during nonproductive time and results in a much lower rate of machine breakdown and failure than in the United States.

Pressure for elimination of defects makes itself felt not in maintenance schedules but in the relationships of producers with suppliers and in work practices on the line. Just-in-time production does not permit extensive inspection of incoming parts. Suppliers must, therefore, maintain consistently high levels of quality, and workers must have the authority to stop operations if they spot defects or other production problems.

Worker-initiated line stoppages are central to the concept of *Jidoka* (making a just-surfaced problem visible to everyone by bringing operations to a halt), which—along with Kanban—helps direct energy and attention to elimination of waste, discovery of problems, and conservation of resources.

It is difficult, of course, to separate the effects of Kanban-Jidoka on process yield from the effects of, say, job structure and quality systems —factors given a somewhat lower ranking by the experts we consulted (see *Exhibit V*). It is also difficult to separate them from the benefits of having a loyal work force (Japanese factories have little unexcused absenteeism). Taken together, these aspects of work force management clearly account for much of the Japanese advantage in production.

It is sometimes argued, by the way, that the union-management relationship in the United States helps explain the superior Japanese performance in productivity and product quality. There is no doubt that the industrial relations system in the U.S. auto industry is a critical element

2. See Robert H. Hayes, "Why Japanese Factories Work," HBR July-August 1981, p. 56.

Exhibit III

Ratings of body and mechanical repair frequency
average = 10; maximum = 20; minimum = 0

Make all models	Body 1980	Mechanical 1980
Domestic		
Buick	9.3	9.4
Chevrolet	8.4	8.9
Dodge	10.0	10.0
Ford	7.2	9.2
Lincoln	8.1	8.4
Oldsmobile	8.4	9.3
Volkswagen	11.3	8.6
Imports		
Datsun	15.3	10.8
Honda	16.0	11.1
Mazda	17.5	12.7
Toyota	16.9	12.4
Volkswagen	11.3	10.0
Volvo	11.9	10.5

Source:
Consumer Reports annual auto issue, April 1981.

Note:
The data cover repair frequency of mechanical systems, components, and body (structure and finish). Ratings are given in five categories: average, below average, far below average, above average, and far above average. Beginning with a score of zero for far below average, we have assigned values of 5, 10, 15, and 20 to the other categories. The sum of the scores on body and mechanical systems gives the total score.

Exhibit IV

Customer loyalty
percent who would buy same make/model again

	Domestic	Imports	Total
Subcompact	77.2	91.6	81.2
Compact	74.2	91.4	72.4
Midsize	75.3	94.5	76.9
Standard	81.8	–	–
Luxury	86.6	94.6	87.2
Weighted average	78.7	91.8	–

Source:
Rogers National Research, *Buyer Profiles*, 1979.

in its performance. Nor is there any doubt that many aspects of that system do not square with the new facts of competitive life. Yet to lay these problems at the door of the union—and only there—is misleading.

Employment contracts and collective bargaining relationships do not just happen. Indeed, a contract provision that a company today finds dysfunctional often was initiated by management some time in the past. Moreover, the production

Exhibit V	Seven factors affecting productivity: comparison of technology, management, and organization	
Factor, with ranking and relative weights	**Definition**	**Comparative practice,** Japan relative to United States
Process systems		
Process yield 1 (40%)	Output rate variations in conventional manufacturing lines; good parts per hour from a line, press, work group, or process line. Key determinants are machine cycle times, system uptime and reliability, affected by materials control methods, maintenance practices, and operating patterns.	Production-materials control minimizes inventory, reduces scrap, exposes problems. Line stops highlight problems and help eliminate defects. Operators perform routine maintenance; scheduling of two shifts instead of three leaves time for better maintenance.
Quality systems 5 (9%)	Series of controls and inspection plans to ensure that products are built to specifications.	Japanese use fewer inspectors. Some authority and responsibility are vested in production worker and supervisor; good relationship with supplier and very high standards lead to less incoming inspection.
Technology		
Process automation 4 (10%)	Introduction and adaptation of advanced, state-of-the-art manufacturing equipment.	Overall, state of technology is comparable. Japanese use more robots; their stamping facilities appear somewhat more automated than average U.S. facilities.
Product design 6 (7%)	Differences in the way the car is designed for a given market segment; aspects affecting productivity: tolerances, number of parts, fastening methods, etc.	Japanese have more experience in small car production and have emphasized design for manufacturability (i.e., productivity and quality). Newer U.S. models (Escort, GM J-car) are first models with design/ manufacturing specifications comparable to Japanese.
Work force management		
Absenteeism 3 (12%)	All employee time away from the workplace, including excused, unexcused, medical, personal, contractual, and other reasons.	Levels of contractual time off are comparable; unexcused absences are much higher in United States.
Job structure 2 (18%)	Tasks and responsibilities included in job definitions.	Japanese practice is to create jobs with more breadth (more tasks or skill per job) and depth (more involvement in planning and control of operations); labor classifications are broader; regular production workers perform more skilled tasks; management layers are fewer.
Work pace 7 (4%)	Speed at which operators perform tasks.	Evidence is inconclusive; some lines run faster, some appear to run more slowly.

philosophy embodied in a contract may have had its origins in the very early days of the industry, long before unionization. Finally, many of the systems and practices that inhibit performance have little to do with a collective bargaining agreement.

Superior manufacturing performance, the key to the Japanese producers' competitive success, is therefore not the fruit of government policy, technical hardware, or national culture (Quadrants 1, 2, and 3). Instead it derives simply from the way people and operations are organized and managed (Quadrant 4).

Technological renewal

Having looked at causes, we now turn our attention to cures. In a time of expensive energy, by their success in the marketplace Japanese producers have rekindled interest in the automobile —especially the small, fuel-efficient automobile—as a product and thus have opened the way for technology to become the relevant basis of competition in the American market. As one General Motors executive remarked, "We took a look at the Honda Accord and we knew that the game had changed."

But does the American auto industry —or, for that matter, do government bureaucrats, lenders, and suppliers—really understand that the game has changed? Our investigation indicates that it has not—yet. We often hear two interpretations of the current crisis, both of them deeply flawed. By extension, both of these interpretations can apply to other sectors of the U.S. industrial economy.

Misperceptions of causes

The first of these interpretations, which we call "the natural consequences of maturity," holds that what has happened is the natural consequence of life cycle processes operating internationally on mature industrial sectors. Once an industry reaches the point where its production process has been embodied in equipment available for purchase—that is, once its mode of production is stable and well known—the location of factories

3. Edward M. Graham, "Technological Innovation and the Dynamics of the U.S. Competitive Advantage in International Trade," in *Technological Innovation for a Dynamic Economy*, edited by Christopher T. Hill and James M. Utterback (Elmsford, N.Y.: Pergamon Press, 1979), p. 152.

becomes a simple matter of exploiting geographic advantages in the relative costs of production. In this view, it makes perfect sense to move these facilities out of the United States as lower cost opportunities become available elsewhere.

Many economists argue that rather than coming to the aid of threatened industries, government and management should follow the path of least resistance, so to speak, and let the life cycle work its will. They recommend a policy not of intervention but, in the phrase of Edward M. Graham, of "positive adjustment." "Government should not," he writes, "protect or subsidize industries that are threatened by imports or [are otherwise] noncompetitive internationally, but should take concrete steps to encourage the transfer of resources from less into more competitive industries."[3]

The question of who is sufficiently infallible to be entrusted with the nasty job of picking winners and losers is, of course, conveniently left unanswered. The evidence to date suggests that no one is.

The second line of interpretation, which we call "transient economic misfortune," is a considerably more optimistic point of view. It holds that the present difficulties with automobiles are temporary, the result of rapid changes in oil prices and consumer preferences. Cost or quality is not the problem, but inappropriate capacity: too many facilities for building big cars.

The forces needed to right the competitive balance are even now locked into place, their happy result merely a matter of time and of bringing the needed capacity on line. Understandably, this view of things appealed strongly to many in the Carter administration, who could use it to rationalize a firm policy of doing nothing.

Both of these interpretive schemes are inadequate—not only because they ignore differences in Quadrant 4 management but also because they count on future stability in technology. Adherents of the maturity thesis assume an irreversible tendency of products to become standardized—that is, technologically stable over time. Adherents of the misfortune thesis, assuming that all outstanding technological problems have been solved, see the industry as needing only to bring the requisite capacity on line to recapture its competitive standing.

Both groups of adherents argue from a set of familiar but outdated assumptions about the relation of technology to industrial development. Looking back on the years since World War II as a period of competition in autos based mainly on economies of scale, styling, and service networks, they persist in viewing the car manufacturers as constituting a typical mature industry, in which

| Exhibit VI | **Determinants of process yield** |

Rated machine speed total parts per hour	x	**Uptime** hours per year	x	**1-defect rate** good parts/ total parts	=	**Annual output of good parts**

any innovation is incremental, never radical, and is thus—in marketing terms—virtually invisible.

Fluidity versus stability

Times have changed. Environmental concerns and the escalating price of oil have combined since the oil shock of 1979 to change the structure of market demand fundamentally. Technological innovation—in its radical as well as its incremental forms—again has vital competitive significance.

Changes in product technology have become at once more rapid and more extreme. Unlike most of the postwar period, recent technical advances have spawned a marked diversity in available systems and components. In engines alone, the once dominant V-8 has been joined by engines with four, five, and six cylinders, diesel engines, rotary engines, and engines with turbocharging and computer feedback control.

Moreover, these kinds of product innovation are increasingly radical in their effects on production processes. We have moved from a period in which product innovation focused on the refinement and extension of existing concepts to a period in which completely new concepts are developed and introduced. And this transition from a time of little change in production systems to a time of great turbulence in equipment, processes, skills, and organization is only beginning.

If our assessment is right, this shift in the nature of innovation will have far-reaching implications for the structure of the industry, the strategic decisions of companies, and the character of international trade. The supposedly mature auto industry now has the opportunity to embark on a technology-based process of rejuvenation in which the industry could recover the open-ended dynamics of its youth when competitive advantage was based largely on the ability to innovate.

Research has shown that manufacturing processes, no less than the products turned out, go through a life cycle evolution. As products evolve from low-volume, unstandardized, one-of-a-kind items toward high-volume, standardized, commoditylike items, the associated processes likewise evolve from individual job-shop production toward continuous-flow production. In other words, a product-process configuration, or productive unit that is initially fluid (relatively inefficient, flexible, and open to radical change), gradually becomes stable (relatively efficient, inflexible, and open only to incremental change).

This seemingly inexorable movement toward technological stability has long been the fate of the auto industry. Economies of scale on massive production lines have for more than a generation dictated the search for ever-greater product standardization and more streamlined production. Radical change in the underlying technology of either became competitively dysfunctional; the production unit was too finely tuned to wring out the last increment of marginal cost reduction—and its management too focused on organizational coordination and control—to allow the entrepreneurially fertile disruptions caused by radically new technology.[4]

The new industrial competition, however, has dated this older logic by rewarding the ability to compete on technological grounds. It has precipitated a technological ferment, which has in turn been supported by the market's post-1979 willingness to pay a premium for vehicles boasting new technology.

Consider, for example, the rapid market adoption of General Motors' X-bodies with their transaxle and transverse mounted engines; the popularity of enhanced four-cylinder engines like Ford's compound-valve hemispherical head; or the appeal of such fuel-saving materials as graphite fibers, dual-phased steel, and advanced plastics. As a result, the industry has begun to revitalize itself in a movement back to a more fluid process-product configuration in the companies and a more lively technology-based competition among them.

Technology-driven strategies

Three factors are the prime elements in the renewal of the auto industry: (1) an increasing premium in the marketplace on innovation, (2) a growing diversity in the technology of components and production processes, and (3) an increasingly radical effect of factors 1 and 2 on long-established configurations in the productive unit as a whole. These developments, in turn, have begun to define the structure and competitive dynamics of the industry in the years ahead—and the corporate strategies best suited to both.

The conventional wisdom about industry structure and strategy accepts an implicit equation between concentration and maturity.

When technology-based competition heats up, this logic runs, industry concentration loosens. In such a case, car manufacturers will know how to adjust their strategies accordingly.

To be sure, in a capital-intensive industry with great economies of scale, a period of ferment in product technology often allows manufacturers to offer an increasing variety of products at or below the cost of the old product mix. Especially when the production technology is well understood and easily procurable (in the form of equipment or human skills), companies on the fringe of the industry and fresh entrants can identify and exploit new market niches. Technological activity, market growth, and industry deconcentration usually go hand in hand.

When, however, the ferment in product technology is so extreme that it causes fundamental alterations in process technology, the same degree of activity may have very different results. In this case the immediate effect of a process-linked industry renewal may well be to *increase* the degree and the stability of concentration—that is, as many believe, to push industry structure apparently in the direction of *greater* maturity.

Where these observers go wrong is in failing to distinguish concentration from maturity or, said another way, in assuming that all evidence of frozen or rising concentration is evidence of movement toward maturity. This may, but need not, be the case.

In the auto field, for example, some corporate responses to the prospect of radical process innovation probably will take the industry farther along the road to maturity. Because truly radical product changes are still some years off and because commitments to existing process technology are large (especially in the standard model segment), it is reasonable to expect producers with experience in the older technologies to defend their positions through technical alterations that reduce costs or improve performance but do not make their processes obsolete.

Such a strategy requires the high volumes necessary for scale economies. As a result, the strategy may help concentrate production—either through greater use of joint ventures or, if the scale effects are great enough, through mergers and like forms of mature industry consolidation.

4. For a discussion of the evolution toward industrial maturity, see James M. Utterback and William J. Abernathy, "A Dynamic Model of Process and Product Innovation," *Omega*, vol. 3, 1975, p. 639.

5. Alfred P. Sloan, Jr., *My Years with General Motors* (Garden City, N.Y.: Doubleday, 1964), pp. 186-187.

Other corporate responses to process-linked renewal may have the opposite effect. Major innovations in products that are linked to innovations in process technology often permit drastic reductions in production costs or improvements in performance, thus making possible the higher volumes necessary to expand market share. These innovations, however, usually involve large capital outlays as well as development of hard-to-acquire skills on the part of workers and management. So they require large increases in volume to offset the greater investment. As a result, only the leading producers may be able to profit from the process innovations and thus, temporarily at least, enhance their market share and reinforce industry concentration.

Though this pattern of concentration may appear identical to the one we have described, nothing could be further from the truth. Here a consolidation of the market serves to throw the industry into technological ferment that stimulates further technological competition—not to lock it into older process technology.

In time, this upheaval in process technology may even provide the competitive basis for new entrants to the field. Depending on the nature of process advances in auto production, companies in related industries (electronics, for example, or engines or energy) may find invasion of the market an attractive strategic option. But even if a decade from now these new entrants have not materialized, the forces that made their participation possible will have changed the competitive structure of the industry in two fundamental ways:

Whatever its immediate tendency, industry concentration will in the long run have become far less stable than at present.

The basis of competition will have changed to reflect the now-crucial importance of technology-driven strategies.

The challenge to management

Once U.S. auto manufacturers understand that energy prices and internationalization of competition have altered the industry's old competitive dynamics, they have to decide how they want to compete under the new rules of the game. It may be best for them to avoid duplicating the Japanese pattern of competition. At any rate, after decades of the maturing process, the basis for competing is in flux for U.S. producers and radical rethinking about strategy—not blind imitation—is in order.

The industrial landscape in America is littered with the remains of once-successful companies that could not adapt their strategic vision to altered conditions of competition. If the automobile producers prove unequal to the new reality that confronts them, their massive, teeming plants will become the ghost towns of late twentieth century America. The same, of course, holds true for all companies, large and small, in those old-line manufacturing industries exposed to assault from abroad. Only those able to see the new industrial competition for what it is and to devise appropriate strategies for participating in it will survive.

Managers must recognize that they have entered a period of competition that requires of them a technology-driven strategy, a mastery of efficient production, and an unprecedented capacity for work force management. They cannot simply copy what others do but must find their own way. No solutions are certain, no strategies assured of success. But the nature of the challenge is clear.

Henry Ford, as Alfred P. Sloan recalled him, was a man who had had "...many brilliant insights in [his] earlier years, [but] seemed never to understand how completely the market had changed from the one in which he had made his name and to which he was accustomed.... The old master failed to master change."[5] That is still the crucial challenge—and opportunity.

See next page for Appendix

Appendix:
The Japanese cost advantage

Table A **Calculation of U.S. and Japanese labor costs for a subcompact vehicle**

	1	2	3	4	5	6 [4 x 5]	7 [6 x .575]
	Share in OEM manufacturing costs	Average OEM hours per vehicle	Estimated OEM employee cost per hour	Estimated cost per vehicle	Labor content	Labor cost per vehicle	U.S.-Japan difference
OEM labor Hourly	.24	65	$ 18	$ 1,170	100 %	$ 1,170	$ 673
Salaried	.08	15	21	315	100	315	181
Purchased components	.39	NA	NA	1,901	66	1,255	721
Purchased materials	.14	NA	NA	683	25	171	98
Total	–	–	–	**$ 4,875**	**NA**	**$ 2,911**	**$ 1,673**

Notes:

OEM hourly labor is defined as total nonexempt and includes direct and indirect production workers. The calculations assume an exchange rate of 218 yen per dollar. The method of calculation and sources of data are as follows:

Column 1 contains estimates of the share of total manufacturing cost accounted for by direct and indirect production labor (at the OEM level), purchased components, and materials. These estimates do not reflect the experience of any one company but approximate an industry average. They are based on data prepared for the National Research Council's Committee on Motor Vehicle Emissions as well as on discussions with industry sources. The latter have also provided us with the data in columns 2, 3, and 5.

We made the calculation of U.S.-Japan cost differences in three steps. We first used the data in columns 2 and 3 to get an OEM labor cost per vehicle of $1,170, then extrapolated using the cost shares (column 1) to arrive at a total manufactured cost and the cost of purchased components and materials (column 4). We next multiplied the cost per vehicle in column 4 by an estimate of the labor content of the three categories presented in column 5. The data imply, for example, that $1,255 of the $1,901 cost of components is labor cost. Finally, we calculated the Japan-U.S. labor cost gap by multiplying the U.S. data in column 6 by 0.575, the adjustment factor derived from our estimate of the Japan-to-U.S. unit labor cost ratio.* Thus column 7 provides an estimate of the difference in the cost of producing a subcompact vehicle in the United States and Japan due to differences in unit labor costs, not only at the OEM level but also at the supplier level.

*Let C(US) and C(J) indicate unit labor costs in the United States and Japan. We estimate C(J)/C(US) = .425. We want to know C(US)−C(J). Column 6 gives us C(US). Thus, C(US)−C(J) = $\left(1 - \dfrac{C(J)}{C(US)}\right)$ x column 6; this result is in column 7.

Table B **Ford and Toyo Kogyo's estimated per-vehicle employee costs in 1979**

	Ford	Toyo Kogyo
Domestic car and truck production* in millions	3.163	0.983
Total domestic employment‡		
Automotive	219,599	24,318
Nonautomotive	19,876	2,490
Total domestic employee hours‡		
Automotive in millions	355.75	46.20
Total employee cost§		
Automotive in millions	$ 7,794.50	$ 482.20
Employee hours per vehicle	112.5	47.0
Employee cost per vehicle	$ 2,464	$ 491

*Ford figure excludes 65,000 imported vehicles; Toyo Kogyo figure is adjusted for production of knock-down assembly kits.

‡Data on automotive employment and costs were obtained by assuming that the ratio of automotive employment to total employment was the same as the ratio of sales. The same assumption was made to obtain Ford employment costs.

‡Ford hours were determined by assuming that each employee worked 1,620 hours per year; Toyo Kogyo hours assume 1,900 hours. These adjustments reflect vacations, holidays, leaves, and absences.

§Data include salaries, wages, and fringe benefits. Toyo Kogyo compensation data were derived by updating a 1976 figure using compensation growth rates at Toyota. An exchange rate of 218 yen/$ (1979 average) was used to convert yen.

Table C	Product mix adjustment		
		Ford	Toyo Kogyo
1.	Ratio of car to total vehicle production	0.645	0.652
2.	Production shares by size		
	Small	0.11	0.83
	Medium	0.68	0.17
	Large	0.21	–
3.	Relative manufacturing cost by size		
	Small	1.00	NA
	Medium	1.35	NA
	Large	1.71	NA
4.	Weighted average of relative manufacturing cost small = 1.00	1.38	1.06
5.	Production of Toyo Kogyo mix at Ford level of integration		
	Employee cost per vehicle	$ 1,893	$ 589
	Employee hours per vehicle	87	56

Notes:

Line 2 for Ford assumes that only Pinto and Bobcat models are small; Mustang and Capri sales were placed in the medium category.

Line 5 for Ford is obtained by multiplying lines 6 and 7 in *Exhibit B* by (1.06/1.38).

Table B uses the data on manufacturing costs by vehicle size developed for the Committee on Motor Vehicle Emissions of the National Research Council in 1974. We derived estimates of the cost to Ford of producing the Toyo Kogyo mix by first computing a weighted average of the relative manufacturing cost indices with Ford's 1979 production shares by size as weights. The ratio of the comparable Toyo Kogyo weighted average (1.06) to the Ford weighted average (1.38) was used to adjust both costs and productivity as a means of estimating the effect of product mix on Ford's average cost and labor hours per vehicle. After these adjustments we estimate that Ford would require 87 employee hours to produce the average-size vehicle in the Toyo Kogyo product line, compared with 56 hours in the Japanese company. Labor cost per vehicle is just over $1,300 higher at Ford. These comparisons are based on the average-size vehicle at Toyo Kogyo. For a small vehicle (i.e., Pinto vs. Mazda GLC), the Ford estimate is 82 hours per vehicle, while the comparable Toyo Kogyo figure is 53; the corresponding costs per vehicle are $1,785 (Ford) and $566 (Toyo Kogyo). Even this adjustment may overstate costs and hours required to produce the Toyo Kogyo mix at Ford if the trucks and commercial vehicles produced by the two companies differ substantially.

Implementing and
Managing Change

Harvard Business Review

Larry E. Greiner

Evolution and revolution as organizations grow

*A company's past has clues for management
that are critical to future success*

Foreword

This author maintains that growing organizations move through five distinguishable phases of development, each of which contains a relatively calm period of growth that ends with a management crisis. He argues, moreover, that since each phase is strongly influenced by the previous one, a management with a sense of its own organization's history can anticipate and prepare for the next developmental crisis. This

article provides a prescription for appropriate management action in each of the five phases, and it shows how companies can turn organizational crises into opportunities for future growth.

Mr. Greiner is Associate Professor of Organizational Behavior at the Harvard Business School and is the author of several previous HBR articles on organization development.

Asmall research company chooses too complicated and formalized an organization structure for its young age and limited size. It flounders in rigidity and bureaucracy for several years and is finally acquired by a larger company.

Key executives of a retail store chain hold on to an organization structure long after it has served its purpose, because their power is derived

from this structure. The company eventually goes into bankruptcy.

A large bank disciplines a "rebellious" manager who is blamed for current control problems, when the underlying cause is centralized pro-

Author's note: This article is part of a continuing project on organization development with my colleague, Professor Louis B. Barnes, and sponsored by the Division of Research, Harvard Business School.

cedures that are holding back expansion into new markets. Many younger managers subsequently leave the bank, competition moves in, and profits are still declining.

The problems of these companies, like those of many others, are rooted more in past decisions than in present events or outside market dynamics. Historical forces do indeed shape the future growth of organizations. Yet management, in its haste to grow, often overlooks such critical developmental questions as: Where has our organization been? Where is it now? And what do the answers to these questions mean for where we are going? Instead, its gaze is fixed outward toward the environment and the future—as if more precise market projections will provide a new organizational identity.

Companies fail to see that many clues to their future success lie within their own organizations and their evolving states of development. Moreover, the inability of management to understand its organization development problems can result in a company becoming "frozen" in its present stage of evolution or, ultimately, in failure, regardless of market opportunities.

My position in this article is that the future of an organization may be less determined by outside forces than it is by the organization's history. In stressing the force of history on an organization, I have drawn from the legacies of European psychologists (their thesis being that individual behavior is determined primarily by previous events and experiences, not by what lies ahead). Extending this analogy of individual development to the problems of organization development, I shall discuss a series of developmental phases through which growing companies tend to pass. But, first, let me provide two definitions:

1. The term *evolution* is used to describe pro-

longed periods of growth where no major upheaval occurs in organization practices.

2. The term *revolution* is used to describe those periods of substantial turmoil in organization life.

As a company progresses through developmental phases, each evolutionary period creates its own revolution. For instance, centralized practices eventually lead to demands for decentralization. Moreover, the nature of management's solution to each revolutionary period determines whether a company will move forward into its next stage of evolutionary growth. As I shall show later, there are at least five phases of organization development, each characterized by both an evolution and a revolution.

Key forces in development

During the past few years a small amount of research knowledge about the phases of organization development has been building. Some of this research is very quantitative, such as time-series analyses that reveal patterns of economic performance over time.[1] The majority of studies, however, are case-oriented and use company records and interviews to reconstruct a rich picture of corporate development.[2] Yet both types of research tend to be heavily empirical without attempting more generalized statements about the overall process of development.

A notable exception is the historical work of Alfred D. Chandler, Jr., in his book *Strategy and Structure*.[3] This study depicts four very broad and general phases in the lives of four large U.S. companies. It proposes that outside market opportunities determine a company's strategy, which in turn determines the company's organization structure. This thesis has a valid ring for the four companies examined by Chandler, largely because they developed in a time of explosive markets and technological advances. But more recent evidence suggests that organization structure may be less malleable than Chandler assumed; in fact, structure can play a critical role in influencing corporate strategy. It is this reverse emphasis on how organization structure affects future growth which is highlighted in the model presented in this article.

From an analysis of recent studies,[4] five key dimensions emerge as essential for building a model of organization development:

1. Age of the organization.

1. See, for example, William H. Starbuck, "Organizational Metamorphosis," in *Promising Research Directions*, edited by R.W. Millman and M.P. Hottenstein (Tempe, Arizona, Academy of Management, 1968), p. 113.

2. See, for example, the *Grangesberg* case series, prepared by C. Roland Christensen and Bruce R. Scott, Case Clearing House, Harvard Business School.

3. *Strategy and Structure: Chapters in the History of the American Industrial Enterprise* (Cambridge, Massachusetts, The M.I.T. Press, 1962).

4. I have drawn on many sources for evidence: (a) numerous cases collected at the Harvard Business School; (b) *Organization Growth and Development*, edited by William H. Starbuck (Middlesex, England, Penguin Books, Ltd., 1971), where several studies are cited; and (c) articles published in journals, such as Lawrence E. Fouraker and John M. Stopford, "Organization Structure and the Multinational Strategy," *Administrative Science Quarterly*, Vol. 13, No. 1, 1968, p. 47; and Malcolm S. Salter, "Management Appraisal and Reward Systems," *Journal of Business Policy*, Vol. 1, No. 4, 1971.

2. Size of the organization.
3. Stages of evolution.
4. Stages of revolution.
5. Growth rate of the industry.

I shall describe each of these elements separately, but first note their combined effect as illustrated in *Exhibit I*. Note especially how each dimension influences the other over time; when all five elements begin to interact, a more complete and dynamic picture of organizational growth emerges.

After describing these dimensions and their interconnections, I shall discuss each evolutionary/revolutionary phase of development and show (a) how each stage of evolution breeds its own revolution, and (b) how management solutions to each revolution determine the next stage of evolution.

Age of the organization

The most obvious and essential dimension for any model of development is the life span of an organization (represented as the horizontal axis in *Exhibit I*). All historical studies gather data from various points in time and then make comparisons. From these observations, it is evident that the same organization practices are not maintained throughout a long time span. This makes a most basic point: management problems and principles are rooted in time. The concept of decentralization, for example, can have meaning for describing corporate practices

Exhibit I. Model of organization development

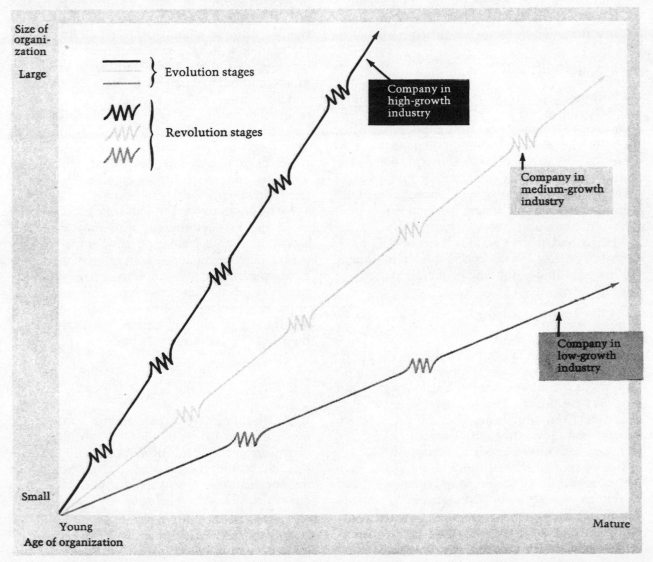

at one time period but loses its descriptive power at another.

The passage of time also contributes to the institutionalization of managerial attitudes. As a result, employee behavior becomes not only more predictable but also more difficult to change when attitudes are outdated.

Size of the organization

This dimension is depicted as the vertical axis in *Exhibit I*. A company's problems and solutions tend to change markedly as the number of employees and sales volume increase. Thus, time is not the only determinant of structure; in fact, organizations that do not grow in size can retain many of the same management issues and practices over lengthy periods. In addition to increased size, however, problems of coordination and communication magnify, new functions emerge, levels in the management hierarchy multiply, and jobs become more interrelated.

Stages of evolution

As both age and size increase, another phenomenon becomes evident: the prolonged growth that I have termed the evolutionary period. Most growing organizations do not expand for two years and then retreat for one year; rather, those that survive a crisis usually enjoy four to eight years of continuous growth without a major economic setback or severe internal disruption. The term evolution seems appropriate for describing these quieter periods because only modest adjustments appear necessary for maintaining growth under the same overall pattern of management.

Stages of revolution

Smooth evolution is not inevitable; it cannot be assumed that organization growth is linear. *Fortune*'s "500" list, for example, has had significant turnover during the last 50 years. Thus we find evidence from numerous case histories which reveals periods of substantial turbulence spaced between smoother periods of evolution.

I have termed these turbulent times the periods of revolution because they typically exhibit a serious upheaval of management practices. Traditional management practices, which were appropriate for a smaller size and earlier time, are brought under scrutiny by frustrated top managers and disillusioned lower-level managers. During such periods of crisis, a number of companies fail—those unable to abandon past practices and effect major organization changes are likely either to fold or to level off in their growth rates.

The critical task for management in each revolutionary period is to find a new set of organization practices that will become the basis for managing the next period of evolutionary growth. Interestingly enough, these new practices eventually sow their own seeds of decay and lead to another period of revolution. Companies therefore experience the irony of seeing a major solution in one time period become a major problem at a latter date.

Growth rate of the industry

The speed at which an organization experiences phases of evolution and revolution is closely related to the market environment of its industry. For example, a company in a rapidly expanding market will have to add employees rapidly; hence, the need for new organization structures to accommodate large staff increases is accelerated. While evolutionary periods tend to be relatively short in fast-growing industries, much longer evolutionary periods occur in mature or slowly growing industries.

Evolution can also be prolonged, and revolutions delayed, when profits come easily. For instance, companies that make grievous errors in a rewarding industry can still look good on their profit and loss statements; thus they can avoid a change in management practices for a longer period. The aerospace industry in its infancy is an example. Yet revolutionary periods still occur, as one did in aerospace when profit opportunities began to dry up. Revolutions seem to be much more severe and difficult to resolve when the market environment is poor.

Phases of growth

With the foregoing framework in mind, let us now examine in depth the five specific phases of evolution and revolution. As shown in *Exhibit II*, each evolutionary period is characterized by the dominant *management style* used to achieve growth, while each revolutionary period is characterized by the dominant *management problem* that must be solved before growth can continue. The patterns presented in *Exhibit II* seem to be

Exhibit II. The five phases of growth

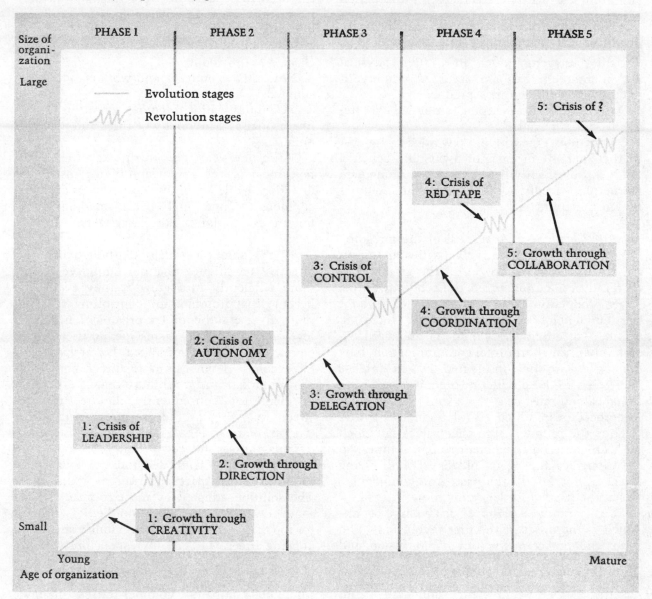

typical for companies in industries with moderate growth over a long time period; companies in faster growing industries tend to experience all five phases more rapidly, while those in slower growing industries encounter only two or three phases over many years.

It is important to note that *each phase is both an effect of the previous phase and a cause for the next phase.* For example, the evolutionary management style in Phase 3 of the exhibit is "delegation," which grows out of, and becomes the solution to, demands for greater "autonomy" in the preceding Phase 2 revolution. The style of delegation used in Phase 3, however, eventually provokes a major revolutionary crisis that is characterized by attempts to regain control over the diversity created through increased delegation.

The principal implication of each phase is that management actions are narrowly prescribed if growth is to occur. For example, a company experiencing an autonomy crisis in Phase 2 cannot return to directive management for a solution—it must adopt a new style of delegation in order to move ahead.

Phase 1: Creativity . . .

In the birth stage of an organization, the emphasis is on creating both a product and a market. Here are the characteristics of the period of creative evolution:

○ The company's founders are usually technically or entrepreneurially oriented, and they disdain management activities; their physical and mental energies are absorbed entirely in making and selling a new product.

○ Communication among employees is frequent and informal.

○ Long hours of work are rewarded by modest salaries and the promise of ownership benefits.

○ Control of activities comes from immediate marketplace feedback; the management acts as the customers react.

. . .& the leadership crisis: All of the foregoing individualistic and creative activities are essential for the company to get off the ground. But therein lies the problem. As the company grows, larger production runs require knowledge about the efficiencies of manufacturing. Increased numbers of employees cannot be managed exclusively through informal communication; new employees are not motivated by an intense dedication to the product or organization. Additional capital must be secured, and new accounting procedures are needed for financial control.

Thus the founders find themselves burdened with unwanted management responsibilities. So they long for the "good old days," still trying to act as they did in the past. And conflicts between the harried leaders grow more intense.

At this point a crisis of leadership occurs, which is the onset of the first revolution. Who is to lead the company out of confusion and solve the managerial problems confronting it? Quite obviously, a strong manager is needed who has the necessary knowledge and skill to introduce new business techniques. But this is easier said than done. The founders often hate to step aside even though they are probably temperamentally unsuited to be managers. So here is the first critical developmental choice— to locate and install a strong business manager who is acceptable to the founders and who can pull the organization together.

Phase 2: Direction . . .

Those companies that survive the first phase by installing a capable business manager usually embark on a period of sustained growth under able and directive leadership. Here are the characteristics of this evolutionary period:

○ A functional organization structure is in-

troduced to separate manufacturing from marketing activities, and job assignments become more specialized.

○ Accounting systems for inventory and purchasing are introduced.

○ Incentives, budgets, and work standards are adopted.

○ Communication becomes more formal and impersonal as a hierarchy of titles and positions builds.

○ The new manager and his key supervisors take most of the responsibility for instituting direction, while lower-level supervisors are treated more as functional specialists than as autonomous decision-making managers.

. . .& the autonomy crisis: Although the new directive techniques channel employee energy more efficiently into growth, they eventually become inappropriate for controlling a larger, more diverse and complex organization. Lower-level employees find themselves restricted by a cumbersome and centralized hierarchy. They have come to possess more direct knowledge about markets and machinery than do the leaders at the top; consequently, they feel torn between following procedures and taking initiative on their own.

Thus the second revolution is imminent as a crisis develops from demands for greater autonomy on the part of lower-level managers. The solution adopted by most companies is to move toward greater delegation. Yet it is difficult for top managers who were previously successful at being directive to give up responsibility. Moreover, lower-level managers are not accustomed to making decisions for themselves. As a result, numerous companies flounder during this revolutionary period, adhering to centralized methods while lower-level employees grow more disenchanted and leave the organization.

Phase 3: Delegation . . .

The next era of growth evolves from the successful application of a decentralized organization structure. It exhibits these characteristics:

○ Much greater responsibility is given to the managers of plants and market territories.

○ Profit centers and bonuses are used to stimulate motivation.

○ The top executives at headquarters restrain themselves to managing by exception, based on periodic reports from the field.

○ Management often concentrates on making

new acquisitions which can be lined up beside other decentralized units.

○ Communication from the top is infrequent, usually by correspondence, telephone, or brief visits to field locations.

The delegation stage proves useful for gaining expansion through heightened motivation at lower levels. Decentralized managers with greater authority and incentive are able to penetrate larger markets, respond faster to customers, and develop new products.

. . . & the control crisis: A serious problem eventually evolves, however, as top executives sense that they are losing control over a highly diversified field operation. Autonomous field managers prefer to run their own shows without coordinating plans, money, technology, and manpower with the rest of the organization. Freedom breeds a parochial attitude.

Hence, the Phase 3 revolution is under way when top management seeks to regain control over the total company. Some top managements attempt a return to centralized management, which usually fails because of the vast scope of operations. Those companies that move ahead find a new solution in the use of special coordination techniques.

Phase 4: Coordination . . .

During this phase, the evolutionary period is characterized by the use of formal systems for achieving greater coordination and by top executives taking responsibility for the initiation and administration of these new systems. For example:

○ Decentralized units are merged into product groups.

○ Formal planning procedures are established and intensively reviewed.

○ Numerous staff personnel are hired and located at headquarters to initiate companywide programs of control and review for line managers.

○ Capital expenditures are carefully weighed and parceled out across the organization.

○ Each product group is treated as an investment center where return on invested capital is an important criterion used in allocating funds.

○ Certain technical functions, such as data processing, are centralized at headquarters, while daily operating decisions remain decentralized.

○ Stock options and companywide profit shar-

ing are used to encourage identity with the firm as a whole.

All of these new coordination systems prove useful for achieving growth through more efficient allocation of a company's limited resources. They prompt field managers to look beyond the needs of their local units. While these managers still have much decision-making responsibility, they learn to justify their actions more carefully to a "watchdog" audience at headquarters.

. . . & the red-tape crisis: But a lack of confidence gradually builds between line and staff, and between headquarters and the field. The proliferation of systems and programs begins to exceed its utility; a red-tape crisis is created. Line managers, for example, increasingly resent heavy staff direction from those who are not familiar with local conditions. Staff people, on the other hand, complain about uncooperative and uninformed line managers. Together both groups criticize the bureaucratic paper system that has evolved. Procedures take precedence over problem solving, and innovation is dampened. In short, the organization has become too large and complex to be managed through formal programs and rigid systems. The Phase 4 revolution is under way.

Phase 5: Collaboration . . .

The last observable phase in previous studies emphasizes strong interpersonal collaboration in an attempt to overcome the red-tape crisis. Where Phase 4 was managed more through formal systems and procedures, Phase 5 emphasizes greater spontaneity in management action through teams and the skillful confrontation of interpersonal differences. Social control and self-discipline take over from formal control. This transition is especially difficult for those experts who created the old systems as well as for those line managers who relied on formal methods for answers.

The Phase 5 evolution, then, builds around a more flexible and behavioral approach to management. Here are its characteristics:

○ The focus is on solving problems quickly through team action.

○ Teams are combined across functions for task-group activity.

○ Headquarters staff experts are reduced in number, reassigned, and combined in interdisciplinary teams to consult with, not to direct, field units.

○ A matrix-type structure is frequently used to assemble the right teams for the appropriate problems.

○ Previous formal systems are simplified and combined into single multipurpose systems.

○ Conferences of key managers are held frequently to focus on major problem issues.

○ Educational programs are utilized to train managers in behavioral skills for achieving better teamwork and conflict resolution.

○ Real-time information systems are integrated into daily decision making.

○ Economic rewards are geared more to team performance than to individual achievement.

○ Experiments in new practices are encouraged throughout the organization.

... & the ? crisis: What will be the revolution in response to this stage of evolution? Many large U.S. companies are now in the Phase 5 evolutionary stage, so the answers are critical. While there is little clear evidence, I imagine the revolution will center around the "psychological saturation" of employees who grow emotionally and physically exhausted by the intensity of teamwork and the heavy pressure for innovative solutions.

My hunch is that the Phase 5 revolution will be solved through new structures and programs that allow employees to periodically rest, reflect, and revitalize themselves. We may even see companies with dual organization structures: a "habit" structure for getting the daily work done, and a "reflective" structure for stimulating perspective and personal enrichment. Employees could then move back and forth between the two structures as their energies are dissipated and refueled.

One European organization has implemented just such a structure. Five reflective groups have been established outside the regular structure for the purpose of continuously evaluating five task activities basic to the organization. They report directly to the managing director, although their reports are made public throughout the organization. Membership in each group includes all levels and functions, and employees are rotated through these groups on a six-month basis.

Other concrete examples now in practice include providing sabbaticals for employees, moving managers in and out of "hot spot" jobs, establishing a four-day workweek, assuring job security, building physical facilities for relaxation *during* the working day, making jobs more interchangeable, creating an extra team on the assembly line so that one team is always off for reeducation, and switching to longer vacations and more flexible working hours.

The Chinese practice of requiring executives to spend time periodically on lower-level jobs may also be worth a nonideological evaluation. For too long U.S. management has assumed that career progress should be equated with an upward path toward title, salary, and power. Could it be that some vice presidents of marketing might just long for, and even benefit from, temporary duty in the field sales organization?

Implications of history

Let me now summarize some important implications for practicing managers. First, the main features of this discussion are depicted in *Exhibit III*, which shows the specific management actions that characterize each growth phase. These actions are also the solutions which ended each preceding revolutionary period.

In one sense, I hope that many readers will react to my model by calling it obvious and natural for depicting the growth of an organization. To me this type of reaction is a useful test of the model's validity.

But at a more reflective level I imagine some of these reactions are more hindsight than foresight. Those experienced managers who have been through a developmental sequence can empathize with it now, but how did they react when in the middle of a stage of evolution or revolution? They can probably recall the limits of their own developmental understanding at that time. Perhaps they resisted desirable changes or were even swept emotionally into a revolution without being able to propose constructive solutions. So let me offer some explicit guidelines for managers of growing organizations to keep in mind.

Know where you are in the developmental sequence.

Every organization and its component parts are at different stages of development. The task of top management is to be aware of these stages; otherwise, it may not recognize when the time for change has come, or it may act to impose the wrong solution.

Exhibit III. Organization practices during evolution in the five phases of growth

Category	PHASE 1	PHASE 2	PHASE 3	PHASE 4	PHASE 5
MANAGEMENT FOCUS	Make & sell	Efficiency of operations	Expansion of market	Consolidation of organization	Problem solving & innovation
ORGANIZATION STRUCTURE	Informal	Centralized & functional	Decentralized & geographical	Line-staff & product groups	Matrix of **teams**
TOP MANAGEMENT STYLE	Individualistic & entrepreneurial	Directive	Delegative	Watchdog	Participative
CONTROL SYSTEM	Market results	Standards & cost centers	Reports & profit centers	Plans & investment centers	Mutual goal setting
MANAGEMENT REWARD EMPHASIS	Ownership	Salary & merit increases	Individual bonus	Profit sharing & stock options	Team bonus

Top leaders should be ready to work with the flow of the tide rather than against it; yet they should be cautious, since it is tempting to skip phases out of impatience. Each phase results in certain strengths and learning experiences in the organization that will be essential for success in subsequent phases. A child prodigy, for example, may be able to read like a teenager, but he cannot behave like one until he ages through a sequence of experiences.

I also doubt that managers can or should act to avoid revolutions. Rather, these periods of tension provide the pressure, ideas, and awareness that afford a platform for change and the introduction of new practices.

Recognize the limited range of solutions.

In each revolutionary stage it becomes evident that this stage can be ended only by certain specific solutions; moreover, these solutions are different from those which were applied to the problems of the preceding revolution. Too often it is tempting to choose solutions that were tried before, which makes it impossible for a new phase of growth to evolve.

Management must be prepared to dismantle current structures before the revolutionary stage becomes too turbulent. Top managers, realizing that their own managerial styles are no longer appropriate, may even have to take themselves out of leadership positions. A good Phase 2 manager facing Phase 3 might be wise to find another Phase 2 organization that better fits his talents, either outside the company or with one of its newer subsidiaries.

Finally, evolution is not an automatic affair; it is a contest for survival. To move ahead, companies must consciously introduce planned structures that not only are solutions to a current crisis but also are fitted to the *next* phase of growth. This requires considerable self-awareness on the part of top management, as well as great interpersonal skill in persuading other managers that change is needed.

Realize that solutions breed new problems.

Managers often fail to realize that organizational solutions create problems for the future (i.e., a decision to delegate eventually causes a problem of control). Historical actions are very much determinants of what happens to the company at a much later date.

An awareness of this effect should help managers to evaluate company problems with greater historical understanding instead of "pinning the blame" on a current development. Better yet, managers should be in a position to *predict* future problems, and thereby to prepare solutions and coping strategies before a revolution gets out of hand.

A management that is aware of the problems ahead could well decide *not* to grow. Top managers may, for instance, prefer to retain the informal practices of a small company, knowing that this way of life is inherent in the organization's limited size, not in their congenial personalities. If they choose to grow, they may do themselves out of a job and a way of life they enjoy.

And what about the managements of very large organizations? Can they find new solutions for continued phases of evolution? Or are they reaching a stage where the government will act to break them up because they are too large.

Concluding note

Clearly, there is still much to learn about processes of development in organizations. The phases outlined here are only five in number and are still only approximations. Researchers are just beginning to study the specific developmental problems of structure, control, rewards, and management style in different industries and in a variety of cultures.

One should not, however, wait for conclusive evidence before educating managers to think and act from a developmental perspective. The critical dimension of time has been missing for too long from our management theories and practices. The intriguing paradox is that by learning more about history we may do a better job in the future.

Choosing strategies for change

In a rapidly changing world managers need to increase their skills at diagnosing resistance to change and at choosing the appropriate methods for overcoming it

John P. Kotter and Leonard A. Schlesinger

"From the frying pan into the fire," "let sleeping dogs lie," and "you can't teach an old dog new tricks" are all well-known sayings born of the fear of change. When people are threatened with change in organizations, similar maxims about certain people and departments are trotted out to prevent an alteration in the status quo. Fear of change is understandable, but because the environment changes rapidly, and it has been doing so increasingly, organizations cannot afford not to change. One major task of a manager, then, is to implement change, and that entails overcoming resistance to it. In this article, the authors describe four basic reasons people resist change. They also describe various methods for dealing with the resistance and provide a guide to what kinds of approaches will work when the different types of resistance occur.

Mr. Kotter is associate professor of business administration at the Harvard Business School. His most recent books include *Self Assessment and Career Development* (with Victor Faux and Charles McArthur, Prentice-Hall, 1978), as well as *Power in Management* (AMACOM, 1979). Mr. Schlesinger is assistant professor in organizational behavior at the Harvard Business School. He and Mr. Kotter are coauthors, with Vijay Sathe, of *Organization* (Richard D. Irwin, to be published in 1979) and *Managing the Human Organization* (Dow Jones–Irwin, 1979).

"It must be considered that there is nothing more difficult to carry out, nor more doubtful of success, nor more dangerous to handle, than to initiate a new order of things."[1]

In 1973, The Conference Board asked 13 eminent authorities to speculate what significant management issues and problems would develop over the next 20 years. One of the strongest themes that runs through their subsequent reports is a concern for the ability of organizations to respond to environmental change. As one person wrote: "It follows that an acceleration in the rate of change will result in an increasing need for reorganization. Reorganization is usually feared, because it means disturbance of the status quo, a threat to people's vested interests in their jobs, and an upset to established ways of doing things. For these reasons, needed reorganization is often deferred, with a resulting loss in effectiveness and an increase in costs."[2]

Subsequent events have confirmed the importance of this concern about organizational change. Today, more and more managers must deal with new government regulations, new products, growth, increased competition, technological developments, and a changing work force. In response, most companies or divisions of major corporations find that they must undertake moderate organizational changes at least once a year and major changes every four or five.[3]

Author's note: This article is adapted from a chapter in a forthcoming Dow Jones–Irwin book. We wish to thank Vijay Sathe for his help in preparing the article.

Editor's note: All references are listed at the end of this article on pages 113 and 114.

Few organizational change efforts tend to be complete failures, but few tend to be entirely successful either. Most efforts encounter problems; they often take longer than expected and desired, they sometimes kill morale, and they often cost a great deal in terms of managerial time or emotional upheaval. More than a few organizations have not even tried to initiate needed changes because the managers involved were afraid that they were simply incapable of successfully implementing them.

In this article, we first describe various causes for resistance to change and then outline a systematic way to select a strategy and set of specific approaches for implementing an organizational change effort. The methods described are based on our analyses of dozens of successful and unsuccessful organizational changes.

Diagnosing resistance

Organizational change efforts often run into some form of human resistance. Although experienced managers are generally all too aware of this fact, surprisingly few take time before an organizational change to assess systematically who might resist the change initiative and for what reasons. Instead, using past experiences as guidelines, managers all too often apply a simple set of beliefs—such as "engineers will probably resist the change because they are independent and suspicious of top management." This limited approach can create serious problems. Because of the many different ways in which individuals and groups can react to change, correct assessments are often not intuitively obvious and require careful thought.

Of course, all people who are affected by change experience some emotional turmoil. Even changes that appear to be "positive" or "rational" involve loss and uncertainty.[4] Nevertheless, for a number of different reasons, individuals or groups can react very differently to change—from passively resisting it, to aggressively trying to undermine it, to sincerely embracing it.

To predict what form their resistance might take, managers need to be aware of the four most common reasons people resist change. These include: a desire not to lose something of value, a misunderstanding of the change and its implications, a belief that the change does not make sense for the organization, and a low tolerance for change.

Parochial self-interest

One major reason people resist organizational change is that they think they will lose something of value as a result. In these cases, because people focus on their own best interests and not on those of the total organization, resistance often results in "politics" or "political behavior."[5] Consider these two examples:

☐ After a number of years of rapid growth, the president of an organization decided that its size demanded the creation of a new staff function—New Product Planning and Development—to be headed by a vice president. Operationally, this change eliminated most of the decision-making power that the vice presidents of marketing, engineering, and production had over new products. Inasmuch as new products were very important in this organization, the change also reduced the vice presidents' status which, together with power, was very important to them.

During the two months after the president announced his idea for a new product vice president, the existing vice presidents each came up with six or seven reasons the new arrangement might not work. Their objections grew louder and louder until the president shelved the idea.

☐ A manufacturing company had traditionally employed a large group of personnel people as counselors and "father confessors" to its production employees. This group of counselors tended to exhibit high morale because of the professional satisfaction they received from the "helping relationships" they had with employees. When a new performance appraisal system was installed, every six months the counselors were required to provide each employee's supervisor with a written evaluation of the employee's "emotional maturity," "promotional potential," and so forth.

As some of the personnel people immediately recognized, the change would alter their relationships from a peer and helper to more of a boss and evaluator with most of the employees. Predictably, the personnel counselors resisted the change. While publicly arguing that the new system was not as good for the company as the old one, they privately put as much pressure as possible on the personnel vice president until he significantly altered the new system.

Political behavior sometimes emerges before and during organizational change efforts when what is in the best interests of one individual or group is not in the best interests of the total organization or of other individuals and groups.

While political behavior sometimes takes the form of two or more armed camps publicly fighting things out, it usually is much more subtle. In many cases, it occurs completely under the surface of public dialogue. Although scheming and ruthless individuals sometimes initiate power struggles, more often than not those who do are people who view their potential loss from change as an unfair violation of their implicit, or psychological, contract with the organization.[6]

Misunderstanding & lack of trust

People also resist change when they do not understand its implications and perceive that it might cost them much more than they will gain. Such situations often occur when trust is lacking between the person initiating the change and the employees.[7] Here is an example:

□ When the president of a small midwestern company announced to his managers that the company would implement a flexible working schedule for all employees, it never occurred to him that he might run into resistance. He had been introduced to the concept at a management seminar and decided to use it to make working conditions at his company more attractive, particularly to clerical and plant personnel.

Shortly after the announcement, numerous rumors begin to circulate among plant employees—none of whom really knew what flexible working hours meant and many of whom were distrustful of the manufacturing vice president. One rumor, for instance, suggested that flexible hours meant that most people would have to work whenever their supervisors asked them to—including evenings and weekends. The employee association, a local union, held a quick meeting and then presented the management with a nonnegotiable demand that the flexible hours concept be dropped. The president, caught completely by surprise, complied.

Few organizations can be characterized as having a high level of trust between employees and managers; consequently, it is easy for misunderstandings to develop when change is introduced. Unless managers surface misunderstandings and clarify them rapidly, they can lead to resistance. And that resistance can easily catch change initiators by surprise, especially if they assume that people only resist change when it is not in their best interest.

Different assessments

Another common reason people resist organizational change is that they assess the situation differently from their managers or those initiating the change and see more costs than benefits resulting from the change, not only for themselves but for their company as well. For example:

□ The president of one moderate-size bank was shocked by his staff's analysis of the bank's real estate investment trust (REIT) loans. This complicated analysis suggested that the bank could easily lose up to $10 million, and that the possible losses were increasing each month by 20%. Within a week, the president drew up a plan to reorganize the part of the bank that managed REITs. Because of his concern for the bank's stock price, however, he chose not to release the staff report to anyone except the new REIT section manager.

The reorganization immediately ran into massive resistance from the people involved. The group sentiment, as articulated by one person, was: "Has he gone mad? Why in God's name is he tearing apart this section of the bank? His actions have already cost us three very good people [who quit], and have crippled a new program we were implementing [which the president was unaware of] to reduce our loan losses."

Managers who initiate change often assume both that they have all the relevant information required to conduct an adequate organization analysis and that those who will be affected by the change have the same facts, when neither assumption is correct. In either case, the difference in information that groups work with often leads to differences in analyses, which in turn can lead to resistance. Moreover, if the analysis made by those not initiating the change is more accurate than that derived by the initiators, resistance is obviously "good" for the organization. But this likelihood is not obvious to some managers who assume that resistance is always bad and therefore always fight it.[8]

Low tolerance for change

People also resist change because they fear they will not be able to develop the new skills and behavior that will be required of them. All human beings are limited in their ability to change, with some people much more limited than others.[9] Organizational change can inadvertently require people to change too much, too quickly.

Peter F. Drucker has argued that the major obstacle to organizational growth is managers' inability to change their attitudes and behavior as rapidly as their organizations require.[10] Even when managers intellectually understand the need for changes in the way they operate, they sometimes are emotionally unable to make the transition.

It is because of people's limited tolerance for change that individuals will sometimes resist a change even when they realize it is a good one. For example, a person who receives a significantly more important job as a result of an organizational change will probably be very happy. But it is just as possible for such a person to also feel uneasy and to resist giving up certain aspects of the current situation. A new and very different job will require new and different behavior, new and different relationships, as well as the loss of some satisfactory current activities and relationships. If the changes are significant and the individual's tolerance for change is low, he might begin actively to resist the change for reasons even he does not consciously understand.

People also sometimes resist organizational change to save face; to go along with the change would be, they think, an admission that some of their previous decisions or beliefs were wrong. Or they might resist because of peer group pressure or because of a supervisor's attitude. Indeed, there are probably an endless number of reasons why people resist change.[11]

Assessing which of the many possibilities might apply to those who will be affected by a change is important because it can help a manager select an appropriate way to overcome resistance. Without an accurate diagnosis of possibilities of resistance, a manager can easily get bogged down during the change process with very costly problems.

Dealing with resistance

Many managers underestimate not only the variety of ways people can react to organizational change, but also the ways they can positively influence specific individuals and groups during a change. And, again because of past experiences, managers sometimes do not have an accurate understanding of the advantages and disadvantages of the methods with which they *are* familiar.

Education & communication

One of the most common ways to overcome resistance to change is to educate people about it beforehand. Communication of ideas helps people see the need for and the logic of a change. The education process can involve one-on-one discussions, presentations to groups, or memos and reports. For example:

□ As a part of an effort to make changes in a division's structure and in measurement and reward systems, a division manager put together a one-hour audiovisual presentation that explained the changes and the reasons for them. Over a four-month period, he made this presentation no less than a dozen times to groups of 20 or 30 corporate and division managers.

An education and communication program can be ideal when resistance is based on inadequate or inaccurate information and analysis, especially if the initiators need the resistors' help in implementing the change. But some managers overlook the fact that a program of this sort requires a good relationship between initiators and resistors or that the latter may not believe what they hear. It also requires time and effort, particularly if a lot of people are involved.

Participation & involvement

If the initiators involve the potential resistors in some aspect of the design and implementation of the change, they can often forestall resistance. With a participative change effort, the initiators listen to the people the change involves and use their advice. To illustrate:

□ The head of a small financial services company once created a task force to help design and implement changes in his company's reward system. The task force was composed of eight second- and third-level managers from different parts of the company. The president's specific charter to them was that they recommend changes in the company's benefit package. They were given six months and asked to file a brief progress report with the president once a month. After they had made their recommendations, which the president largely accepted, they were asked to help the company's personnel director implement them.

We have found that many managers have quite strong feelings about participation—sometimes positive and sometimes negative. That is, some managers feel that there should always be participation during change efforts, while others feel this is virtually always a mistake. Both attitudes can create problems for a manager, because neither is very realistic.

When change initiators believe they do not have all the information they need to design and implement a change, or when they need the whole-hearted commitment of others to do so, involving others makes very good sense. Considerable research has demonstrated that, in general, participation leads to commitment, not merely compliance.[12] In some instances, commitment is needed for the change to be a success. Nevertheless, the participation process does have its drawbacks. Not only can it lead to a poor solution if the process is not carefully managed, but also it can be enormously time consuming. When the change must be made immediately, it can take simply too long to involve others.

Facilitation & support

Another way that managers can deal with potential resistance to change is by being supportive. This process might include providing training in new skills, or giving employees time off after a demanding period, or simply listening and providing emotional support. For example:

□ Management in one rapidly growing electronics company devised a way to help people adjust to frequent organizational changes. First, management staffed its human resource department with four counselors who spent most of their time talking to people who were feeling "burnt out" or who were having difficulty adjusting to new jobs. Second, on a selective basis, management offered people four-week minisabbaticals that involved some reflective or educational activity away from work. And, finally, it spent a great deal of money on in-house education and training programs.

Facilitation and support are most helpful when fear and anxiety lie at the heart of resistance. Seasoned, tough managers often overlook or ignore this kind of resistance, as well as the efficacy of facilitative ways of dealing with it. The basic drawback of this approach is that it can be time consuming and expensive and still fail.[13] If time, money, and patience just are not available, then using supportive methods is not very practical.

Negotiation & agreement

Another way to deal with resistance is to offer incentives to active or potential resistors. For instance, management could give a union a higher wage rate in return for a work rule change; it could increase an individual's pension benefits in return for an early retirement. Here is an example of negotiated agreements:

□ In a large manufacturing company, the divisions were very interdependent. One division manager wanted to make some major changes in his organization. Yet, because of the interdependence, he recognized that he would be forcing some inconvenience and change on other divisions as well. To prevent top managers in other divisions from undermining his efforts, the division manager negotiated a written agreement with each. The agreement specified the outcomes the other division managers would receive and when, as well as the kinds of cooperation that he would receive from them in return during the change process. Later, whenever the division managers complained about his changes or the change process itself, he could point to the negotiated agreements.

Negotiation is particularly appropriate when it is clear that someone is going to lose out as a result of a change and yet his or her power to resist is significant. Negotiated agreements can be a relatively easy way to avoid major resistance, though, like some other processes, they may become expensive. And once a manager makes it clear that he will negotiate to avoid major resistance, he opens himself up to the possibility of blackmail.[14]

Manipulation & co-optation

In some situations, managers also resort to covert attempts to influence others. Manipulation, in this context, normally involves the very selective use of information and the conscious structuring of events.

One common form of manipulation is co-optation. Co-opting an individual usually involves giving him or her a desirable role in the design or implementation of the change. Co-opting a group involves giving one of its leaders, or someone it respects, a key role in the design or implementation of a change. This is not a form of participation, however, because the initiators do not want the advice of the co-opted, merely his or her endorsement. For example:

□ One division manager in a large multibusiness corporation invited the corporate human relations vice president, a close friend of the president, to

Exhibit I
Methods for dealing with resistance to change

Approach	Commonly used in situations	Advantages	Drawbacks
Education + communication	Where there is a lack of information or inaccurate information and analysis.	Once persuaded, people will often help with the implementation of the change.	Can be very time-consuming if lots of people are involved.
Participation + involvement	Where the initiators do not have all the information they need to design the change, and where others have considerable power to resist.	People who participate will be committed to implementing change, and any relevant information they have will be integrated into the change plan.	Can be very time-consuming if participators design an inappropriate change.
Facilitation + support	Where people are resisting because of adjustment problems.	No other approach works as well with adjustment problems.	Can be time-consuming, expensive, and still fail.
Negotiation + agreement	Where someone or some group will clearly lose out in a change, and where that group has considerable power to resist.	Sometimes it is a relatively easy way to avoid major resistance.	Can be too expensive in many cases if it alerts others to negotiate for compliance.
Manipulation + co-optation	Where other tactics will not work, or are too expensive.	It can be a relatively quick and inexpensive solution to resistance problems.	Can lead to future problems if people feel manipulated.
Explicit + implicit coercion	Where speed is essential, and the change initiators possess considerable power.	It is speedy, and can overcome any kind of resistance.	Can be risky if it leaves people mad at the initiators.

help him and his key staff diagnose some problems the division was having. Because of his busy schedule, the corporate vice president was not able to do much of the actual information gathering or analysis himself, thus limiting his own influence on the diagnoses. But his presence at key meetings helped commit him to the diagnoses as well as the solutions the group designed. The commitment was subsequently very important because the president, at least initially, did not like some of the proposed changes. Nevertheless, after discussion with his human relations vice president, he did not try to block them.

Under certain circumstances co-optation can be a relatively inexpensive and easy way to gain an individual's or a group's support (cheaper, for example, than negotiation and quicker than participation). Nevertheless, it has its drawbacks. If people feel they are being tricked into not resisting, are not being treated equally, or are being lied to, they may respond very negatively. More than one manager has found that, by his effort to give some subordinate a sense of participation through co-optation, he created more resistance than if he had done nothing. In addition, co-optation can create a different kind of problem if those co-opted use their ability to influence the design and implementation of changes in ways that are not in the best interests of the organization.

Other forms of manipulation have drawbacks also, sometimes to an even greater degree. Most people are likely to greet what they perceive as covert treatment and/or lies with a negative response. Furthermore, if a manager develops a reputation as a manipulator, it can undermine his ability to use needed approaches such as education/communication and participation/involvement. At the extreme, it can even ruin his career.

Nevertheless, people do manipulate others successfully—particularly when all other tactics are not feasible or have failed.[15] Having no other alternative, and not enough time to educate, involve, or support people, and without the power or other resources to negotiate, coerce, or co-opt them, managers have resorted to manipulating information channels in order to scare people into thinking there is a crisis coming which they can avoid only by changing.

Explicit & implicit coercion

Finally, managers often deal with resistance coercively. Here they essentially force people to accept a change by explicitly or implicitly threatening them (with the loss of jobs, promotion possibilities, and so forth) or by actually firing or transferring them. As with manipulation, using coercion is a risky process because inevitably people strongly resent forced change. But in situations where speed is essential and where the changes will not be popular, regardless of how they are introduced, coercion may be the manager's only option.

Successful organizational change efforts are always characterized by the skillful application of a num-

Exhibit II
Strategic continuum

Fast	Slower
Clearly planned.	Not clearly planned at the beginning.
Little involvement of others.	Lots of involvement of others.
Attempt to overcome any resistance.	Attempt to minimize any resistance.

Key situational variables

The amount and type of resistance that is anticipated.

The position of the initiators vis-à-vis the resistors (in terms of power, trust, and so forth).

The locus of relevant data for designing the change, and of needed energy for implementing it.

The stakes involved (e.g., the presence or lack of presence of a crisis, the consequences of resistance and lack of change).

ber of these approaches, often in very different combinations. However, successful efforts share two characteristics: managers employ the approaches with a sensitivity to their strengths and limitations (see *Exhibit I* on preceding page) and appraise the situation realistically.

The most common mistake managers make is to use only one approach or a limited set of them *regardless of the situation*. A surprisingly large number of managers have this problem. This would include the hard-boiled boss who often coerces people, the people-oriented manager who constantly tries to involve and support his people, the cynical boss who always manipulates and co-opts others, the intellectual manager who relies heavily on education and communication, and the lawyerlike manager who usually tries to negotiate.[16]

A second common mistake that managers make is to approach change in a disjointed and incremental way that is not a part of a clearly considered strategy.

Choice of strategy

In approaching an organizational change situation, managers explicitly or implicitly make strategic choices regarding the speed of the effort, the amount of preplanning, the involvement of others, and the relative emphasis they will give to different approaches. Successful change efforts seem to be those

where these choices both are internally consistent and fit some key situational variables.

The strategic options available to managers can be usefully thought of as existing on a continuum (see *Exhibit II*).[17] At one end of the continuum, the change strategy calls for a very rapid implementation, a clear plan of action, and little involvement of others. This type of strategy mows over any resistance and, at the extreme, would result in a fait accompli. At the other end of the continuum, the strategy would call for a much slower change process, a less clear plan, and involvement on the part of many people other than the change initiators. This type of strategy is designed to reduce resistance to a minimum.[18]

The further to the left one operates on the continuum in *Exhibit II*, the more one tends to be coercive and the less one tends to use the other approaches—especially participation; the converse also holds.

Organizational change efforts that are based on inconsistent strategies tend to run into predictable problems. For example, efforts that are not clearly planned in advance and yet are implemented quickly tend to become bogged down owing to unanticipated problems. Efforts that involve a large number of people, but are implemented quickly, usually become either stalled or less participative.

Situational factors

Exactly where a change effort should be strategically positioned on the continuum in *Exhibit II* depends on four factors:

1. The amount and kind of resistance that is anticipated. All other factors being equal, the greater the anticipated resistance, the more difficult it will be simply to overwhelm it, and the more a manager will need to move toward the right on the continuum to find ways to reduce some of it.[19]

2. The position of the initiator vis-à-vis the resistors, especially with regard to power. The less power the initiating manager *must* move to the right on the continuum.[20] Conversely, the stronger the initiator's position, the more he or she can move to the left. position, the more he or she can move to the right.

3. The person who has the relevant data for designing the change and the energy for implementing it. The more the initiators anticipate that they will need information and commitment from others to help design and implement the change, the more they must move to the right.[21] Gaining useful information and commitment requires time and the involvement of others.

4. The stakes involved. The greater the short-run potential for risks to organizational performance and survival if the present situation is not changed, the more one must move to the left.

Organizational change efforts that ignore these factors inevitably run into problems. A common mistake some managers make, for example, is to move too quickly and involve too few people despite the fact that they do not have all the information they really need to design the change correctly.

Insofar as these factors still leave a manager with some choice of where to operate on the continuum, it is probably best to select a point as far to the right as possible for both economic and social reasons. Forcing change on people can have just too many negative side effects over both the short and the long term. Change efforts using the strategies on the right of the continuum can often help develop an organization and its people in useful ways.[22]

In some cases, however, knowing the four factors may not give a manager a comfortable and obvious choice. Consider a situation where a manager has a weak position vis-à-vis the people whom he thinks need a change and yet is faced with serious consequences if the change is not implemented immediately. Such a manager is clearly in a bind. If he somehow is not able to increase his power in the situation, he will be forced to choose some compromise strategy and to live through difficult times.

Implications for managers

A manager can improve his chance of success in an organizational change effort by:

1. Conducting an organizational analysis that identifies the current situation, problems, and the forces that are possible causes of those problems. The analysis should specify the actual importance of the problems, the speed with which the problems must be addressed if additional problems are to be avoided, and the kinds of changes that are generally needed.

2. Conducting an analysis of factors relevant to producing the needed changes. This analysis should focus on questions of who might resist the change, why, and how much; who has information that is needed to design the change, and whose cooperation is essential in implementing it; and what is the position of the initiator vis-à-vis other relevant parties in terms of power, trust, normal modes of interaction, and so forth.

3. Selecting a change strategy, based on the previous analysis, that specifies the speed of change, the amount of preplanning, and the degree of involvement of others; that selects specific tactics for use with various individuals and groups; and that is internally consistent.

4. Monitoring the implementation process. No matter how good a job one does of initially selecting a change strategy and tactics, something unexpected will eventually occur during implementation. Only by carefully monitoring the process can one identify the unexpected in a timely fashion and react to it intelligently.

Interpersonal skills, of course, are the key to using this analysis. But even the most outstanding interpersonal skills will not make up for a poor choice of strategy and tactics. And in a business world that continues to become more and more dynamic, the consequences of poor implementation choices will become increasingly severe.

References

1. Niccolò Machiavelli, *The Prince.*

2. Marvin Bower and C. Lee Walton, Jr., "Gearing a Business to the Future," in *Challenge to Leadership* (New York: The Conference Board, 1973), p. 126.

3. For recent evidence on the frequency of changes, see Stephen A. Allen, "Organizational Choice and General Influence Networks for Diversified Companies," *Academy of Management Journal*, September 1978, p. 341.

4. For example, see Robert A. Luke, Jr., "A Structural Approach to Organizational Change," *Journal of Applied Behavioral Science*, September-October 1973, p. 611.

5. For a discussion of power and politics in corporations, see Abraham Zaleznik and Manfred F.R. Kets de Vries, *Power and the Corporate Mind* (Boston: Houghton Mifflin, 1975), Chapter 6; and Robert H. Miles, *Macro Organizational Behavior* (Pacific Palisades, Calif.: Goodyear, 1978), Chapter 4.

6. See Edgar H. Schein, *Organizational Psychology* (Englewood Cliffs, N.J.: Prentice-Hall, 1965), p. 44.

7. See Chris Argyris, *Intervention Theory and Method* (Reading, Mass.: Addison-Wesley, 1970), p. 70.

8. See Paul R. Lawrence, "How to Deal with Resistance to Change," HBR May–June 1954, p. 49; reprinted as HBR Classic, January–February 1969, p. 4.

9. For a discussion of resistance that is personality based, see Goodwin Watson, "Resistance to Change," in *The Planning of Change*, eds. Warren G. Bennis, Kenneth F. Benne, and Robert Chin (New York: Holt, Rinehart, and Winston, 1969), p. 489.

10. Peter F. Drucker, *The Practice of Management* (New York: Harper and Row, 1954).

11. For a general discussion of resistance and reasons for it, see Chapter 3 in Gerald Zaltman and Robert Duncan, *Strategies for Planned Change* (New York: John Wiley, 1977).

12. See, for example, Alfred J. Marrow, David F. Bowers, and Stanley E. Seashore, *Management by Participation* (New York: Harper and Row, 1967).

13. Zaltman and Duncan, *Strategies for Planned Change*, Chapter 4.

14. For an excellent discussion of negotiation, see Gerald I. Nierenberg, *The Art of Negotiating* (Birmingham, Ala.: Cornerstone, 1968).

15. See John P. Kotter, "Power, Dependence, and Effective Management," HBR July-August 1977, p. 125.

16. Ibid., p. 135.

17. See Larry E. Greiner, "Patterns of Organization Change," HBR May–June 1967, p. 119; and Larry E. Greiner and Louis B. Barnes, "Organization Change and Development," in *Organizational Change and Development*, eds. Gene W. Dalton and Paul R. Lawrence (Homewood, Ill.: Irwin, 1970), p. 3.

18. For a good discussion of an approach that attempts to minimize resistance, see Renato Tagiuri, "Notes on the Management of Change: Implication of Postulating a Need for Competence," in John P. Kotter, Vijay Sathe, and Leonard A. Schlesinger, *Organization* (Homewood, Ill.: Irwin, to be published in 1979).

19. Jay W. Lorsch, "Managing Change," in *Organizational Behavior and Administration*, eds. Paul R. Lawrence, Louis B. Barnes, and Jay W. Lorsch (Homewood, Ill.: Irwin, 1976), p. 676.

20. Ibid.

21. Ibid.

22. Michael Beer, *Organization Change and Development: A Systems View* (Pacific Palisades, Calif., Goodyear, to be published in 1979).

HBR Classic

Paul R. Lawrence

How to deal with resistance to change

The real problem is not technical change but the human changes that often accompany technical innovations

Foreword

This "HBR Classic," one of a series of articles from the past with retrospective commentary, was first published in the May-June 1954 issue of HBR. It has been used and reused by executives and managers ever since; request for reprints, for instance, have continued steadily to this day—evidence that the author's analysis of the problems and of how to deal with them continues to be valid. Mr. Lawrence is still associated with the Harvard Business School, where he is now Wallace Brett Donham Professor of Organizational Behavior.

One of the most baffling and recalcitrant of the problems which business executives face is employee resistance to change. Such resistance may take a number of forms—persistent reduction in output, increase in the number of "quits" and requests for transfer, chronic quarrels, sullen hostility, wildcat or slowdown strikes, and, of course, the expression of a lot of pseudological reasons why the change will not work. Even the more petty forms of this resistance can be troublesome.

All too often when executives encounter resistance to change, they "explain" it by quoting the cliché that "people resist change" and never look further. Yet changes must continually occur in industry. This applies with particular force to the all-important "little" changes that constantly take place—changes in work methods, in routine office procedures, in the location of a machine or a desk, in personnel assignments and job titles.

No one of these changes makes the headlines, but in total they account for much of our increase in productivity. They are not the spectacular once-in-a-lifetime technological revolutions that involve mass layoffs or the obsolescence of traditional skills, but they are vital to business progress.

Does it follow, therefore, that business management is forever saddled with the onerous job of "forcing" change down the throats of resistant people? My answer is *no*. It is the thesis of this article that people do *not* resist technical change as such and that most of the resistance which does occur is unnecessary. I shall discuss these points, among others:

1. A solution which has become increasingly popular for dealing with resistance to change is to get the people involved to "participate" in making the change. But as a practical matter "participation" as a device is not a good way for management to think about the problem. In fact, it may lead to trouble.

2. The key to the problem is to understand the true nature of resistance. Actually, what employees resist is usually not technical change but social change—the change in their human relationships that generally accompanies technical change.

3. Resistance is usually created because of certain blind spots and attitudes which staff special-

ists have as a result of their preoccupation with the technical aspects of new ideas.

4. Management can take concrete steps to deal constructively with these staff attitudes. The steps include emphasizing new standards of performance for staff specialists and encouraging them to think in different ways, as well as making use of the fact that signs of resistance can serve as a practical warning signal in directing and timing technological changes.

5. Top executives can also make their own efforts more effective at meetings of staff and operating groups where change is being discussed. They can do this by shifting their attention from the facts of schedules, technical details, work assignments, and so forth, to what the discussion of these items indicates in regard to developing resistance and receptiveness to change.

Let us begin by taking a look at some research into the nature of resistance to change. There are two studies in particular that I should like to discuss. They highlight contrasting ways of interpreting resistance to change and of coping with it in day-to-day administration.

Is participation enough?

The first study was conducted by Lester Coch and John R.P. French, Jr. in a clothing factory.[1] It deserves special comment because, it seems to me, it is the most systematic study of the phenomenon of resistance to change that has been made in a factory setting. To describe it briefly:

The two researchers worked with four different groups of factory operators who were being paid on a modified piece-rate basis. For each of these four groups a minor change in the work procedure was installed by a different method, and the results were carefully recorded to see what, if any, problems of resistance occurred. The four experimental groups were roughly matched with respect to efficiency ratings and degree of cohesiveness; in each group the proposed change modified the established work procedure to about the same degree.

The work change was introduced to the first group by what the researchers called a "no-participation" method. This small group of op-

erators was called into a room where some staff people told the members that there was a need for a minor methods change in their work procedures. The staff people then explained the change to the operators in detail, and gave them the reasons for the change. The operators were then sent back to the job with instructions to work in accordance with the new method.

The second group of operators was introduced to the work change by a "participation-through-representation" method—a variation of the approach used with the third and fourth groups which turned out to be of little significance.

The third and fourth groups of operators were both introduced to the work change on a "total-participation" basis. All the operators in these groups met with the staff people concerned. The staff people dramatically demonstrated the need for cost reduction. A general agreement was reached that some savings could be effected. The groups then discussed how existing work methods could be improved and unnecessary operations eliminated. When the new work methods were agreed on, all the operators were trained in the new methods, and all were observed by the time-study people for purposes of establishing a new piece rate on the job.

Research findings: The researchers reported a marked contrast between the results achieved by the different methods of introducing this change:

▽ *No-participation group*—The most striking difference was between Group #1, the no-participation group, and Groups #3 and #4, the total-participation groups. The output of Group #1 dropped immediately to about two thirds of its previous output rate. The output rate stayed at about this level throughout the period of 30 days after the change was introduced. The researchers further reported:

"Resistance developed almost immediately after the change occurred. Marked expressions of aggression against management occurred, such as conflict with the methods engineer, . . . hostility toward the supervisor, deliberate restriction of production, and lack of cooperation with the supervisor. There were 17% quits in the first 40 days. Grievances were filed about piece rates;

1. See Lester Coch and John R.P. French, Jr., "Overcoming Resistance to Change," *Human Relations*, Vol. 1, No. 4, 1948, p. 512.

Retrospective commentary

In the 15 years since this article was published, we have seen a great deal of change in industry, but the human aspects of the topic do not seem very different. The human problems associated with change remain much the same even though our understanding of them and our methods for dealing with them have advanced.

The first of the two major themes of the article is that resistance to change does not arise because of technical factors per se but because of social and human considerations. This statement still seems to be true. There is, however, an implication in the article that the social and human costs of change, if recognized, can largely be avoided by thoughtful management effort. Today I am less sanguine about this.

It is true that these costs can be greatly reduced by conscious attention. Managements that have tried have made much progress during the past 15 years. Here are some examples of what has been done:

O Fewer people are now pushed out of the back doors of industry—embittered and "burned out" before their time.

O Fewer major strikes are the result of head-on clashes over new technology and its effects on jobs.

O Progress is being made in putting the needs of people into the design of new technological systems.

O Relevant inputs of ideas and opinions of people from all ranks are being solicited and used *before* (not after) plans for change are frozen.

O At the same time that well-established work groups are disrupted by technical imperatives, special efforts are made to help newly formed work groups evolve meaningful team relations quickly.

O Time and care have been taken to counsel individuals whose careers have to some degree been disrupted by change.

All of these ways of reducing the human costs of change have worked for the companies that have seriously applied them. Still, I am more aware than in 1954 of the limits of such approaches. They do not always enable management to prevent situations from developing in which some individuals win while others lose. The values lost as skills become obsolete cannot always be replaced. The company's earnings may go up but the percentage payouts from even an enlarged "pie" have to be recalculated, and then the relative rewards shift. In these situations enlightened problem solving will not completely displace old-fashioned bargaining, and better communication will only clarify the hard-core realities.

The second theme of the article deals with ways of improving the relations between groups in an organization—particularly when a staff group is initiating change in the work of an operating or line group. The gap that exists in outlook and orientation between specialized groups in industry has increased in the past 15 years, even as the number of such groups has continued to escalate. These larger gaps have in turn created ever more difficult problems of securing effective communication and problem solving between groups. Coordinating the groups is probably the number one problem of our modern corporations. So this second theme is hardly out-of-date.

Today, however, there is both more knowledge available about the problem than there was in 1954 and more sophisticated skill and attention being given to it. And there is increasing understanding of and respect for the necessity for differences between groups. There is less striving for consistency for its own sake. More managerial effort is being applied, in person and through impersonal systems, to bridge the gaps in understanding. While the conflicts between specialized groups are probably as intense now as ever, they are more frequently seen as task-related—that is, natural outgrowths of different jobs, skills, and approaches—rather than as redundant and related only to personality differences.

The major criticism that has been brought to my attention about the article is that it has damaged the useful concept of participation. Perhaps this is true. But the view of participation as a technique for securing compliance with a predetermined change was a widespread and seductive one in 1954—and it is not dead yet. Subsequent research has not altered the general conclusion that participation, to be of value, must be based on a search for ideas that are seen as truly relevant to the change under consideration. The shallow notion of participation, therefore, still needs to be debunked.

As a final thought, I now realize that the article implied that workers resist change while managers foster and implement change. Many of the changes of the intervening period, such as the computer revolution, have exposed the inadequacy of this assumption. It is difficult to find any managers today who do not at times feel greatly distressed because of changes, with their own resistance level running fairly high. We are all, at times, resistors as well as instigators of change. We are all involved on both sides of the process of adjusting to change.

In light of this, let me reemphasize the point that resistance to change is by itself neither good nor bad. Resistance may be soundly based or not. It is always, however, an important signal calling for further inquiry by management.

but when the rate was checked, it was found to be a little 'loose.' "

△ *Total-participation groups* — In contrast with this record, Groups #3 and #4 showed a smaller initial drop in output and a very rapid recovery not only to the previous production rate but to a rate that exceeded the previous rate. In these groups there were no signs of hostility toward the staff people or toward the supervisors, and there were no quits during the experimental period.

Appraisal of results: Without going into all the researchers' decisions based on these experiments, it can be fairly stated that they concluded that resistance to methods changes could be overcome by *getting the people involved in the change to participate in making it.*

This was a very useful study, but the results are likely to leave the manager of a factory still bothered by the question, "Where do we go from here?" The trouble centers around that word "participation." It is not a new word. It is seen often in management journals, heard often in management discussions. In fact, the idea that it is a good thing to get employee participation in making changes has become almost axiomatic in management circles.

But participation is not something that can be conjured up or created artificially. You obviously cannot buy it as you would buy a typewriter. You cannot hire industrial engineers and accountants and other staff people who have the ability "to get participation" built into them. It is doubtful how helpful it would be to call in a group of supervisors and staff people and exhort them, "Get in there and start participation."

Participation is a feeling on the part of people, not just the mechanical act of being called in to take part in discussions. Common sense would suggest that people are more likely to respond to the way they are customarily treated—say, as people whose opinions are respected because they themselves are respected for their own worth—rather than by the stratagem of being called to a meeting or being asked some carefully calculated questions. In fact, many

supervisors and staff have had some unhappy experiences with executives who have read about participation and have picked it up as a new psychological gimmick for getting other people to think they "want" to do as they are told—as a sure way to put the sugar coating on a bitter pill.

So there is still the problem of how to get this thing called participation. And, as a matter of fact, the question remains whether participation was the determining factor in the Coch and French experiment or whether there was something of deeper significance underlying it.

Resistance to what?

Now let us take a look at a second series of research findings about resistance to change. . . . While making some research observations in a factory manufacturing electronic products, a colleague and I had an opportunity to observe a number of incidents that for us threw new light on this matter of resistance to change.[2] One incident was particularly illuminating:

☐ We were observing the work of one of the industrial engineers and a production operator who had been assigned to work with the engineer on assembling and testing an experimental product that the engineer was developing. The engineer and the operator were in almost constant daily contact in their work. It was a common occurrence for the engineer to suggest an idea for some modification in a part of the new product; he would then discuss his idea with the operator and ask her to try out the change to see how it worked. It was also a common occurrence for the operator to get an idea as she assembled parts and to pass this idea on to the engineer, who would then consider it and, on occasion, ask the operator to try out the idea and see if it proved useful.

A typical exchange between these two people might run somewhat as follows:

Engineer: "I got to thinking last night about that difficulty we've been having on assembling the x part in the last few days. It occurred to me

that we might get around that trouble if we washed the part in a cleaning solution just prior to assembling it."

Operator: "Well, that sounds to me like it's worth trying."

Engineer: "I'll get you some of the right kind of cleaning solution, and why don't you try doing that with about 50 parts and keep track of what happens."

Operator: "Sure, I'll keep track of it and let you know how it works."

With this episode in mind, let us take a look at a second episode involving the same production operator. One day we noticed another engineer approaching the production operator. We knew that this particular engineer had had no previous contact with the production operator. He had been asked to take a look at one specific problem on the new product because of his special technical qualifications. He had decided to make a change in one of the parts of the product to eliminate the problem, and he had prepared some of these parts using his new method. Here is what happened:

☐ He walked up to the production operator with the new parts in his hand and indicated to her by a gesture that he wanted her to try assembling some units using his new part. The operator picked up one of the parts and proceeded to assemble it. We noticed that she did not handle the part with her usual care. After she had assembled the product, she tested it and it failed to pass inspection. She turned to the new engineer and, with a triumphant air, said, "It doesn't work."

The new engineer indicated that she should try another part. She did so, and again it did not work. She then proceeded to assemble units using all of the new parts that were available. She handled each of them in an unusually rough manner. None

2. For a complete report of the study, see Harriet O. Ronken and Paul R. Lawrence, *Administering Changes: A Case Study of Human Relations in a Factory* (Boston, Division of Research, Harvard Business School, 1952).

Resistance to change   81

of them worked. Again she turned to the engineer and said that the new parts did not work.

The engineer left, and later the operator, with evident satisfaction, commented to the original industrial engineer that the new engineer's idea was just no good.

Social change: What can we learn from these episodes? To begin, it will be useful for our purposes to think of change as having both a technical and a social aspect. The *technical* aspect of the change is the making of a measurable modification in the physical routines of the job. The *social* aspect of the change refers to the way those affected by it think it will alter their established relationships in the organization.

We can clarify this distinction by referring to the two foregoing episodes. In both of them, the technical aspects of the changes introduced were virtually identical: the operator was asked to use a slightly changed part in assembling the finished product. By contrast, the social aspects of the changes were quite different.

In the first episode, the interaction between the industrial engineer and the operator tended to sustain the give-and-take kind of relationship that these two people were accustomed to. The operator was used to being treated as a person with some valuable skills and knowledge and some sense of responsibility about her work; when the engineer approached her with his idea, she felt

she was being dealt with in the usual way. But, in the second episode, the new engineer was introducing not only a technical change but also a change in the operator's customary way of relating herself to others in the organization. By his brusque manner and by his lack of any explanation, he led the operator to fear that her usual work relationships were being changed. And she just did not like the new way she was being treated.

The results of these two episodes were quite different also. In the first episode there were no symptoms of resistance to change, a very good chance that the experimental change would determine fairly whether a cleaning solution would improve product quality, and a willingness on the part of the operator to accept future changes when the industrial engineer suggested them. In the second episode, however, there were signs of resistance to change (the operator's careless handling of parts and her satisfaction in their failure to work), failure to prove whether the modified part was an improvement or not, and indications that the operator would resist any further changes by the engineer. We might summarize the two contrasting patterns of human behavior in the two episodes in graphic form; see *Exhibit I.*

It is apparent from these two patterns that the variable which determines the result is the *social* aspect of the change. In other words, the

operator did not resist the technical change as such but rather the accompanying change in her human relationships.

Confirmation: This conclusion is based on more than one case. Many other cases in our research project substantiate it. Furthermore, we can find confirmation in the research experience of Coch and French, even though they came out with a different interpretation.

Coch and French tell us in their report that the procedure used with Group #1, i.e., the no-participation group, was the usual one in the factory for introducing work changes. And yet they also tell us something about the customary treatment of the operators in their work life. For example, the company's labor relations policies are progressive, the company and the supervisors place a high value on fair and open dealings with the employees, and the employees are encouraged to take up their problems and grievances with management. Also, the operators are accustomed to measuring the success and failure of themselves as operators against the company's standard output figures.

Now compare these *customary* work relationships with the way the Group #1 operators were treated when they were introduced to this particular work change. There is quite a difference. When the management called them into the room for indoctrination, they were treated as if they had no useful knowledge of their own jobs. In effect, they were told that they were not the skilled and efficient operators they had thought they were, that they were doing the job inefficiently, and that some "outsider" (the staff expert) would now tell them how to do it right. How could they construe this experience *except* as a threatening change in their usual working relationship? It is the story of the second episode in our research case all over again. The results were also the same, with signs of resistance, persistently low output, and so on.

Now consider experimental Groups #3 and #4, i.e., the total-participation groups. Coch and French referred

Exhibit I. Two contrasting patterns of human behavior

	Change		
	Technical aspect	Social aspect	Results
Episode 1	Clean part prior to assembly	Sustaining the customary work relationship of operator	1. No resistance 2. Useful technical result 3. Readiness for more change
Episode 2	Use new part in assembly	Threatening the customary work relationship of operator	1. Signs of resistance 2. No useful technical result 3. Lack of readiness for more change

to management's approach in their case as a "new" method of introducing change; but, from the point of view of the *operators* it must not have seemed new at all. It was simply a continuation of the way they were ordinarily dealt with in the course of their regular work. And what happened? The results—reception to change, technical improvement, better performance—were much like those reported in the first episode between the operator and the industrial engineer.

So the research data of Coch and French tend to confirm the conclusion that the nature and size of the technical aspect of the change does not determine the presence or absence of resistance nearly so much as does the social aspect of the change.

Roots of trouble

The significance of these research findings, from management's point of view, is that executives and staff experts need not expertness in using the devices of participation but a real understanding, in depth and detail, of the specific social arrangements that will be sustained or threatened by the change or by the way in which it is introduced.

These observations check with everyday management experience in industry. When we stop to think about it, we know that many changes occur in our factories without a bit of resistance. We know that people who are working closely with one another continually swap ideas about short cuts and minor changes in procedure that are adopted so easily and naturally that we seldom notice them or even think of them as change. The point is that because these people work so closely with one another, they intuitively understand and take account of the existing social arrangements for work and so feel no threat to themselves in such everyday changes.

By contrast, management actions leading to what we commonly label "change" are usually initiated outside the small work group by staff people. These are the changes that we notice and the ones that most frequently bring on symptoms of re-

sistance. By the very nature of their work, most of our staff specialists in industry do not have the intimate contact with operating groups that allows them to acquire an intuitive understanding of the complex social arrangements which their ideas may affect. Neither do our staff specialists always have the day-to-day dealings with operating people that lead them to develop a natural respect for the knowledge and skill of these people. As a result, all too often the men behave in a way that threatens and disrupts the established social relationships. And the tragedy is that so many of these upsets are inadvertent and unnecessary.

Yet industry must have its specialists—not only many kinds of engineering specialists (product, process, maintenance, quality, and safety engineers) but also cost accountants, production schedulers, purchasing agents, and personnel people. Must top management therefore reconcile itself to continual resistance to change, or can it take constructive action to meet the problem?

I believe that our research in various factory situations indicates why resistance to change occurs and what management can do about it. Let us take the "why" factors first.

Self-preoccupation: All too frequently we see staff specialists who bring to their work certain blind spots that get them into trouble when they initiate change with operating people. One such blind spot is "self-preoccupation." The staff specialists get so engrossed in the technology of the change they are interested in promoting that they become wholly oblivious to different kinds of things that may be bothering people. Here are two examples:

☐ In one situation the staff people introduced, with the best of intentions, a technological change which inadvertently deprived a number of skilled operators of much of the satisfaction that they were finding in their work. Among other things, the change meant that, whereas formerly the operators' outputs had been placed beside their work positions where they could be viewed and appreciated by everyone, they were now

being carried away immediately from their work positions. The workers did not like this.

The sad part of it was that there was no compelling cost or technical reason why the output could not be placed beside the work position as it had been formerly. But the staff people who had introduced the change were so literal-minded about their ideas that when they heard complaints on the changes from the operators, they could not comprehend what the trouble was. Instead, they began repeating all the logical arguments why the change made sense from a cost standpoint. The final result here was a chronic restriction of output and persistent hostility on the part of the operators.

☐ An industrial engineer undertook to introduce some methods changes in one department with the notion firmly in mind that this assignment presented her with an opportunity to "prove" to higher management the value of her function. She became so preoccupied with her personal desire to make a name for her particular techniques that she failed to pay any attention to some fairly obvious and practical considerations which the operating people were calling to her attention but which did not show up in her time-study techniques. As could be expected, resistance quicky developed to all her ideas, and the only "name" that she finally won for her techniques was a black one.

Obviously, in both of these situations the staff specialists involved did not take into account the social aspects of the change they were introducing. For different reasons they got so preoccupied with the technical aspects of the change that they literally could not see or understand what all the fuss was about.

We may sometimes wish that the validity of the technical aspect of the change were the sole determinant of its acceptability. But the fact remains that the social aspect is what determines the presence or absence of resistance. Just as ignoring this fact is the sure way to trouble, so taking advantage of it can lead to positive results. We must not forget that these same social arrangements which at times seem so bothersome are essential for the performance of work. Without a network of established social relationships a factory would be populated with a collection of people who had no idea of how to work with one another in an organized fashion. By working *with* this network instead of *against* it, management's staff representatives can give new technological ideas a better chance of acceptance.

Know-how of operators overlooked: Another blind spot of many staff specialists is to the strengths as well as to the weaknesses of firsthand production experience. They do not recognize that the production foreman and the production operator are in their own way specialists themselves—specialists in actual experience with production problems. This point should be obvious, but it is amazing how many staff specialists fail to appreciate the fact that even though they themselves may have a superior knowledge of the technology of the production process involved, the foreman or the operators may have a more practical understanding of how to get daily production out of a group of workers and machines.

The experience of the operating people frequently equips them to be of real help to staff specialists on at least two counts: (1) The operating people are often able to spot practical production difficulties in the ideas of the specialists—and iron out those difficulties before it is too late; (2) the operating people are often able to take advantage of their intimate acquaintance with the existing social arrangements for getting work done. If given a chance, they can use this kind of knowledge to help detect those parts of the change that will have undesirable social consequences. The staff experts can then go to work on ways to avoid the trouble area without materially affecting the technical worth of the change.

Further, some staff specialists have yet to learn the truth that, even after the plans for a change have been carefully made, it takes *time* to put the change successfully into produc-tion use. Time is necessary even though there may be no resistance to the change itself. The operators must develop the skill needed to use new methods and new equipment efficiently; there are always bugs to be taken out of a new method or piece of equipment even with the best of engineering. When staff people begin to lose patience with the amount of time that these steps take, the workers will begin to feel that they are being pushed; *this* amounts to a change in their customary work relationships, and resistance will start building up where there was none before.

The situation is aggravated if the staff specialist mistakenly accuses the operators of resisting the idea of the change, for there are few things that irritate people more than to be blamed for resisting change when actually they are doing their best to learn a difficult new procedure.

Management action

Many of the problems of resistance to change arise around certain kinds of *attitudes* that staff people are liable to develop about their jobs and their own ideas for introducing change. Fortunately, management can influence these attitudes and thus deal with the problems at their source.

Broadening staff interests: It is fairly common for staff members to work so hard on an idea for change that they come to identify themselves with it. This is fine for the organization when the staff person is working on the idea alone or with close colleagues; the idea becomes "his baby," and the company benefits from this complete devotion to work.

But when, for example, a staff member goes to some group of operating people to introduce a change, his very identification with his ideas tends to make him unreceptive to any suggestions for modification. He just does not feel like letting anyone else tamper with his pet ideas. It is easy to see, of course, how this attitude is interpreted by the operating people as a lack of respect for their suggestions.

This problem of staff peoples' extreme identification with their work is one which, to some extent, can only be cured by time. But here are four suggestions for speeding up the process:

1. Managers can often, with wise timing, encourage the staff's interest in a different project that is just starting.

2. Managers can also, by "coaching" as well as by example, prod the staff people to develop a healthier respect for the contributions they can receive from operating people; success in this area would, of course, virtually solve the problem.

3. It also helps if staff people can be guided to recognize that the satisfaction they derive from being productive and creative is the same satisfaction they deny the operating people by resisting them. Experience shows that staff people can sometimes be stimulated by the thought of finding satisfaction in sharing with others in the organization the pleasures of being creative.

4. Sometimes, too, staff people can be led to see that winning acceptance of their ideas through better understanding and handling of human beings is just as challenging and rewarding as giving birth to an idea.

Using understandable terms: One of the problems that must be overcome arises from the fact that most staff people are likely to have the attitude that the reasons why they are recommending any given change may be so complicated and specialized that it is impossible to explain them to operating people. It may be true that the operating people would find it next to impossible to understand some of the staff specialists' analytical techniques, but this does not keep them from coming to the conclusion that the staff specialists are trying to razzle-dazzle them with tricky figures and formulas—insulting their intelligence—if they do not strive to their utmost to translate their ideas into terms understandable to the operators. The following case illustrates the importance of this point:

☐ A staff specialist was temporarily successful in "selling" a change based on a complicated mathematical formula to a foreman who really did not understand it. The whole thing backfired, however, when the foreman tried to sell it to his operating people. They asked him a couple of sharp questions that he could not answer. His embarrassment about this led him to resent and resist the change so much that eventually the whole proposition fell through. This was unfortunate in terms not only of human relations but also of technological progress in the plant.

There are some very good reasons, both technical and social, why staff people should be interested in working with the operating people until their recommendations make "sense." (This does not mean the the operating people need to understand the recommendations in quite the same way or in the same detail that the staff people do, but that they should be able to visualize the recommendations in terms of their job experiences.) Failure of the staff person to provide an adequate explanation is likely to mean that a job the operators had formerly performed with understanding and satisfaction will now be performed without understanding and with less satisfaction.

This loss of satisfaction not only concerns the individual involved but also is significant from the standpoint of the company that is trying to get maximum productivity from the operating people. People who do not have a feeling of comprehension of what they are doing are denied the opportunity to exercise that uniquely human ability—the ability to use informed and intelligent judgment on what they do. If the staff person leaves the operating people with a sense of confusion, they will also be left unhappy and less productive.

Top line and staff executives responsible for the operation should make it a point, therefore, to know how the staff person goes about installing a change. They can do this by asking discerning questions about staff reports, listening closely to reports of employee reaction, and, if they have the opportunity, actually watching the staff specialist at work. At times they may have to take such drastic action as insisting that the time of installation of a proposed change be postponed until the operators are ready for it. But, for the most part, straight-

forward discussions with the staff specialist evaluating that person's approach should help the staffer over a period of time, to learn what is expected in relationships with operating personnel.

New look at resistance: Another attitude that gets staff people into trouble is the *expectation* that all the people involved will resist the change. It is curious but true that the staff person who goes into a job with the conviction that people are going to resist any new idea with blind stubbornness is likely to find them responding just the way the staff specialist thinks they will. The process is clear: whenever the people who are supposed to buy new ideas are treated as if they were bullheaded, the way they are used to being treated changes; and they *will* be bullheaded in resisting *that* change!

I think that staff people—and management in general—will do better to look at it this way: When resistance *does* appear, it should not be thought of as something to be *overcome*. Instead, it can best be thought of as a useful red flag—a signal that something is going wrong. To use a rough analogy, signs of resistance in a social organization are useful in the same way that pain is useful to the body as a signal that some bodily functions are getting out of adjustment.

The resistance, like the pain, does not tell what is wrong but only that something *is* wrong. And it makes no more sense to try to overcome such resistance than it does to take a pain killer without diagnosing the bodily ailment. Therefore, when resistance appears, it is time to listen carefully to find out what the trouble is. What is needed is not a long harangue on the logics of the new recommendations but a careful exploration of the difficulty.

It may happen that the problem is some technical imperfection in the change that can be readily corrected. More than likely, it will turn out that the change is threatening and upsetting some of the established social arrangements for doing work. Whether the trouble is easy or difficult to correct, management will at least know what it is dealing with.

New job definition: Finally, some staff specialists get themselves in trouble because they assume they have the answer in the thought that people will accept a change when they have participated in making it. For example:

☐ In one plant we visited, an engineer confided to us (obviously because we, as researchers on human relations, were interested in psychological gimmicks!) that she was going to put across a proposed production layout change of hers by inserting in it a rather obvious error, which others could then suggest should be corrected. We attended the meeting where this stunt was performed, and superficially it worked. Somebody caught the error, proposed that it be corrected, and our engineer immediately "bought" the suggestion as a very worthwhile one and made the change. The group then seemed to "buy" his entire layout proposal.

It looked like an effective technique—oh, so easy—until later, when we became better acquainted with the people in the plant. Then we found out that many of the engineer's colleagues considered her a phony and did not trust her. The resistance they put up to her ideas was very subtle, yet even more real and difficult for management to deal with.

Participation will never work so long as it is treated as a device to get other people to do what you want them to. Real participation is based on respect. And respect is not acquired by just trying; it is acquired when the staff people face the reality that they need the contributions of the operating people.

If staff people define their jobs as not just generating ideas but also getting those ideas into practical operation, they will recognize their real dependence on the contributions of the operating people. They will ask the operators for ideas and suggestions, not in a backhanded way to get compliance, but in a straightforward way to get some good ideas and avoid some unnecessary mistakes. By this process staff people will be treating the operating people in such a way that their behavior will not be perceived as a threat to customary work relationships. It will be possible to discuss, and accept or reject, the ideas on their own merit.

The staff specialist who looks at the process of introducing change and at resistance to change in the manner outlined in the preceding pages may not be hailed as a genius, but can be counted on in installing a steady flow of technical changes that will cut costs and improve quality without upsetting the organization.

Role of the administrator

Now what about the way top executives go about their *own* jobs as they involve the introduction of change and problems of resistance?

One of the most important things an executive can do, of course, is to deal with staff people in much the same way that the staff members should deal with the operators. An executive must realize that staff people resist social change, too. (This means, among other things, that particular rules should not be prescribed to staff on the basis of this article!)

But most important, I think, is the way the administrators conceive of their job in coordinating the work of the different staff and line groups involved in a change. Does an administrator think of these duties *primarily* as checking up, delegating and following through, applying pressure when performance fails to measure up? Or does the executive think of them *primarily* as facilitating communication and understanding between people with different points of view—for example, between a staff engineering group and a production group who do not see eye to eye on a change they are both involved in? An analysis of management's actual experience—or, at least, that part of it which has been covered by our research—points to the latter as the more effective concept of administration.

I do not mean that executives should spend their time with the different people concerned discussing the human problems of change as such. They *should* discuss schedules, technical details, work assignments, and so forth. But they should also be watching closely for the messages that are passing back and forth as people discuss these topics. Executives will find that people—themselves as well as others—are always implicitly asking and making answers to questions like: "How will she accept criticism?" "How much can I afford to tell him?" "Does she really get my point?" "Is he playing games?" The answers to such questions determine the degree of candor and the amount of understanding between the people involved.

When administrators concern themselves with these problems and acts to facilitate understanding, there will be less logrolling and more sense of common purpose, fewer words and better understanding, less anxiety and more acceptance of criticism, less griping and more attention to specific problems—in short, better performance in putting new ideas for technological change into effect.

Of boxes, bubbles, and effective management

Managers facing a crisis discover that hard facts (boxes) and soft processes (bubbles) are both necessary to keep a company alive

David K. Hurst

One day in 1980 a group of four managers in a large Canadian steel company found their company acquired by another that had essentially no managerial ranks and few resources. The executives, traditional men accustomed to working with hard facts and solid numbers, found that their "hard box" way of managing did not fit their new topsy-turvy world where financiers were banging on the door, previously healthy divisions were faltering, plants had to be closed down, and the worst recession in years loomed on the horizon. To deal with their new circumstances, the management team, as they came to call themselves, had to adopt another managerial mode as well: the soft bubble of process.

They found that some aspects of business lend themselves to hard box solutions, others to soft bubble resolutions. The difference between the two is great, and the key to effective management is the ability both to determine which context is appropriate for the effort at hand and to "jump out of the box," or rigid belief structures, if necessary. With their new approach the team saved their company from certain disaster. In good times, they now "create a crisis" when one is necessary and infuse even routine activities with importance.

Mr. Hurst is an executive vice president of Russelsteel Inc., a subsidiary of Federal Industries, Ltd., Canada. The other members of the management team involved in the turnaround are Wayne P.E. Mang, president and chief operating officer; Al Shkut, executive vice president; and Michael J. Greene, vice president and secretary-treasurer.

Harvard Business Review
Soldiers Field Road
Boston, Massachusetts 02163

Dear Editors:

We are writing to tell you how events from 1979 on have forced us, a team of four general managers indistinguishable from thousands of others, to change our view of what managers should do. In 1979 we were working for Hugh Russel Inc., the fiftieth largest public company in Canada. Hugh Russel was an industrial distributor with some $535 million in sales and a net income of $14 million. The organization structure was conventional: 16 divisions in four groups, each with a group president reporting to the corporate office. Three volumes of corporate policy manuals spelled out detailed aspects of corporate life, including our corporate philosophy. In short, in 1979 our corporation was like thousands of other businesses in North America.

During 1980, however, through a series of unlikely turns, that situation changed drastically. Hugh Russel found itself acquired in a 100% leveraged buyout and then merged with a large, unprofitable (that's being kind!) steel fabricator, York Steel Construction, Ltd. The resulting entity was York Russel Inc., a privately held company except for the existence of some publicly owned preferred stock which obliged us to report to the public.

As members of the acquired company's corporate office, we waited nervously for the ax to fall. Nothing happened. Finally, after about six weeks, Wayne (now our president) asked the new owner if we could do anything to help the deal along. The new chairman was delighted and gave us complete access to information about the acquirer.

Editor's note: All references are listed at the end of the article.

It soon became apparent that the acquiring organization had little management strength. The business had been run in an entrepreneurial style with hundreds of people reporting to a single autocrat. The business had, therefore, no comprehensive plan and, worse still, no money. The deal had been desperately conceived to shelter our profits from taxes and use the resulting cash flow to fund the excessive debt of the steel fabrication business.

Our first job was to hastily assemble a task force to put together a $300 million bank loan application and a credible turnaround plan. Our four-member management team (plus six others who formed a task force) did it in only six weeks. The merged business, York Russel, ended up with $10 million of equity and $275 million of debt on the eve of a recession that turned out to be the worst Canada had experienced since the Great Depression. It was our job then to save the new company, somehow.

Conceptual frameworks are important aids to managers' perceptions, and every team should have a member who can build them. Before the acquisition, the framework implicit in our organization was a "hard," rational model rather like those Thomas Peters and Robert Waterman describe.[1] Jay Galbraith's elaborate model is one of the purest examples of the structure-follows-strategy school.[2] The model clearly defines all elements and their relationships to each other, presumably so that they can be measured (see the *Exhibit*).

Because circumstances changed after the acquisition, our framework fell apart almost immediately. Overnight we went from working for a growth company to working for one whose only objective was survival. Our old decentralized organization was cumbersome and expensive; our new organization needed cash, not profits. Bankers and suppliers swarmed all over us, and the quiet life of a management-controlled public company was gone.

Compounding our difficulties, the recession quickly revealed all sorts of problems in businesses that up to that time had given us no trouble. Even the core nuggets offered up only meager profits, while interest rates of up to 25% quickly destroyed what was left of the balance sheet.

In the heat of the crisis, the management team jelled quickly. At first each member muddled in his own way, but as time went by, we started to gain a new understanding of how to be effective. Even now we do not completely understand the conceptual framework that has evolved, and maybe we never will. What follows is our best attempt to describe to you and your readers what guides us today.

Yours truly,

The management team

Two models are better than one

The hard, rational model isn't wrong; it just isn't enough. There is something more. As it turns out, there is a great deal more.

At York Russel we have had to develop a "soft," intuitive framework that offers a counterpart to every element in the hard, rational framework. As the exhibit shows and the following sections discuss, in the soft model, roles are the counterparts of tasks, groups replace structure, networks operate instead of information systems, the rewards are soft as opposed to hard, and people are viewed as social animals rather than as rational beings.

That may not sound very new. But we found that the key to effective management of not only our crisis but also the routine is to know whether we are in a hard "box" or a soft "bubble" context. By recognizing the dichotomy between the two, we can choose the appropriate framework.

☐ **Tasks** ...&...	○ **Roles**
☐ *Static*	○ *Fluid*
☐ *Clarity*	○ *Ambiguity*
☐ *Content*	○ *Process*
☐ *Fact*	○ *Perception*
☐ *Science*	○ *Art*

These are some of our favorite words for contrasting these two aspects of management. Here's how we discovered them.

The merger changed our agenda completely. We had new shareholders, a new bank, a new business (the steel fabrication operations consisted of nine divisions), and a new relationship with the managers of our subsidiaries, who were used to being left alone to grow. The recession and high interest rates rendered the corporation insolvent. Bankruptcy loomed large. Further, our previously static way of operating became very fluid.

In general, few of us had clear tasks, and for the most part we saw the future as ambiguous and fearful. We found ourselves describing what we had to do as roles rather than as tasks. At first our descriptions were crude. We talked of having an "inside man" who deals with administration, lawyers, and bankers versus an "outside man" who deals with operations, customers, and suppliers. Some of us were "readers," others "writers," some "talkers," and others "listeners." As the readers studied the work of behavioral science researchers and talked to the listeners, we found some more useful classifications. Henry Mintzberg's description of managers' work in terms of three roles—interpersonal (figurehead, leader, liaison), informational (monitor, disseminator, spokesperson), and decisional—helped us see the variety of the job.[3] Edgar Schein's analysis of group roles helped us concentrate on the process of communication as well as on what was communicated.[4]

The most useful framework we used was the one Ichak Adize developed for decision-making roles.[5] In his view, a successful management team needs to play four distinct parts. The first is that of producer of results. A *producer* is action oriented and knowledgeable in his or her field; he or she helps compile plans with an eye to their implementability. The *administrator* supervises the system and manages the detail. The *entrepreneur* is a creative risk taker who initiates action, comes up with new ideas, and challenges existing policies. And the *integrator* brings people together socially and their ideas intellectually, and interprets the significance of events. The integrator gives the team a sense of direction and shared experience.

According to Adize, each member must have some appreciation of the others' roles (by having some facility in those areas), and it is essential that they get along socially. At York Russel the producers (who typically come out of operations) and administrators (usually accountants) tend to be hard box players, while the entrepreneurs tend to live in the soft bubble. Integrators (friendly, unusually humble MBAs) move between the hard and the soft, and we've found a sense of humor is essential to being able to do that well.

The key to a functioning harmonious group, however, has been for members to understand that they might disagree with each other because they are in two different contexts. Different conceptual frameworks may lead people to different conclusions based on the same facts. Of the words describing tasks and roles, our favorite pair is "fact" versus "perception." People in different boxes will argue with each other over facts, for facts in boxes are compelling—they seem so tangible. Only from the bubble can one see them for what they are: abstractions based on the logical frameworks, or boxes, being used.

☐ **Structure..&..**	○ **Groups**
☐ *Cool*	○ *Warm*
☐ *Formal*	○ *Informal*
☐ *Closed*	○ *Open*
☐ *Obedience*	○ *Trust*
☐ *Independence*	○ *Autonomy*

Our premerger corporation was a pretty cold place to work. Senior management kept control in a tight inner circle and then played hardball (in a hard box, of course) with the group presidents. Managers negotiated budgets and plans on a win-lose basis; action plans almost exclusively controlled what was done in the organization. Top managers kept a lot of information to themselves. People didn't trust each other very much.

The crises that struck the corporation in 1980 were so serious that we could not have concealed them even if we had wanted to. We were forced to put together a multitude of task forces consisting of people from all parts of the organization to address these urgent issues, and in the process, we had to reveal everything we knew, whether it was confidential or not.

We were amazed at the task forces' responses: instead of resigning en masse (the hard box players had said that people would leave the company when they found out that it was insolvent), the teams tackled their projects with passion. Warmth, a sense of belonging, and trust characterized the groups; the more we let them know what was going on, the more we received from them. Confidentiality is the enemy of trust. In the old days strategic plans were stamped "confidential." Now we know that paper plans mean nothing if they are not in the minds of the managers.

Division managers at first resented our intrusion into their formal, closed world. "What happened to independence?" they demanded. We described the soft counterpart—autonomy—to them. Unlike independence, autonomy cannot be granted once and for all. In our earlier life, division personnel told the corporate office what they thought it wanted to hear. "You've got to keep those guys at arm's length" was a typical division belief. An autonomous relationship depends on trust for its nourishment. "The more you level with us," we said, "the more we'll leave you alone." That took some getting used to.

But in the end autonomy worked. We gave division managers confidential information, shared our hopes and fears, and incorporated their views in our bubble. They needed to be helped out of their boxes, not to abandon them altogether but to gain a deeper appreciation of and insight into how they were running their businesses. Few could resist when we walked around showing a genuine interest in their views. Because easy access to each other and opportunities for communication determine how groups form and work together, we encouraged managers to keep their doors open. We called this creation of opportunities for communication by making senior management accessible "management by walking around." Chance encounters should not be left to chance.

Although the primary objective of all this communication is to produce trust among group members, an important by-product is that the integrators among us have started to "see" the communication process.[6] In other words, they are beginning to understand why people say what they say. This ability to "see" communication is elusive at times, but when it is present, it enables us to "jump out of the box"— that is, to talk about the frameworks' supporting conclusions rather than the conclusions themselves. We have defused many potential confrontations and struck many deals by changing the context of the debate rather than the debate itself.[7]

Perhaps the best example of this process was our changing relationship with our lead banker. As the corporation's financial position deteriorated, our relationship with the bank became increasingly adversarial. The responsibility for our account rose steadily up the bank's hierarchy (we had eight different account managers in 18 months), and we received tougher and tougher "banker's speeches" from successively more senior executives. Although we worried a great deal that the bank might call the loan, the real risk was that our good businesses would be choked by overzealous efforts on the part of individual bankers to "hold the line."

Key to our ability to change the relationship was to understand why individuals were taking the positions they were. To achieve that understanding, we had to rely on a network of contacts both inside and outside the bank. We found that the bank had as many views as there were people we talked to. Fortunately, the severity of the recession and the proliferation of corporate loan problems had already blown everyone out of the old policy "boxes." It remained for us to gain the confidence of our contacts, exchange candid views of our positions, and present options that addressed the corporation's problems in the bank's context and dealt with the bank's interests.

The "hard" vehicle for this was the renegotiation of our main financing agreement. During the more than six month negotiating process, our relationship with the bank swung 180 degrees from confrontation to collaboration. The corporation's problem became a joint bank-corporation problem. We had used the bubble to find a new box in which both the corporation and the bank could live.

☐ Information processes...&...○ Networks

☐ Hard	○ Soft
☐ Written	○ Oral
☐ Know	○ Feel
☐ Control	○ Influence
☐ Decision	○ Implementation

Over the years our corporation has developed some excellent information systems. Our EDP facility is second to none in our industry. Before the acquisition and merger, when people talked about or requested information, they meant hard, quantitative data and written reports that would be used for control and decision making. The crisis required that we make significant changes to these systems. Because, for example, we became more interested in cash flow than earnings per share, data had to be aggregated and presented in a new way.

The pivotal change, however, was our need to communicate with a slew of new audiences over which we had little control. For instance, although we still have preferred stock quoted in the public market, our principal new shareholders were family members with little experience in professional management of public companies. Our new bankers were in organizational turmoil themselves and took 18 months to realize the horror of what they had financed. Our suppliers, hitherto benign, faced a stream of bad financial news about us and other members of the industry. The rumor mill had us in receivership on a weekly basis.

Our plant closures and cutbacks across North America brought us into a new relationship with government, unions, and the press. And we had a new internal audience: our employees, who were understandably nervous about the "imminent" bankruptcy.

We had always had some relationship with these audiences, but now we saw what important sources of information they were and expanded these networks vastly.[8] Just as we had informed the division managers at the outset, we decided not to conceal from these other groups the fact that the corporation was insolvent but worthy of support. We made oral presentations supported by formal written material to cover the most important bases.

To our surprise, this candid approach totally disarmed potential antagonists. For instance, major suppliers could not understand why we had told them we were in trouble before the numbers revealed the fact. By the time the entire war story was news, there was no doubt that our suppliers' top managers, who tended not to live in the hard accounting box, were on our side. When their financial specialists concluded that we were insolvent, top management blithely responded, "We've known that for six months."

Sharing our view of the world with constituencies external to the corporation led to other unexpected benefits, such as working in each other's interests. Our reassurance to customers that we would be around to deliver on contracts strengthened the relationship. Adversity truly is opportunity!

Management by walking around was the key to communicating with employees in all parts of the company. As a result of the continual open communication, all employees appreciated the corporation's position. Their support has been most gratifying. One of our best talker-listeners (our president) tells of a meeting with a very nervous group of employees at one facility. After he had spent several hours explaining the company's situation, one blue-collar worker who had been with the company for years took him aside and told him that a group of employees would be prepared to take heavy pay cuts if it would save the business. It turns out that when others hear this story it reinforces *their* belief in the organization.

We have found that sharing our views and incorporating the views of others as appropriate has a curious effect on the making and the implementing of decisions. As we've said, in our previous existence the decisions we made were always backed up by hard information; management was decisive, and that was good. Unfortunately, too few of these "good" decisions ever got implemented. The simple process of making the decision the way we did often set up resistance down the line. As the decision was handed down to consecutive organizational levels, it lost impetus until eventually it was unclear whether the decision was right in the first place.

Now we worry a good deal less about making decisions; they arise as fairly obvious conclusions drawn from a mass of shared assumptions. It's the assumptions that we spend our time working on. One of our "producers" (an executive vice president) calls it "conditioning," and indeed it is. Of course, making decisions this way requires that senior management build networks with people many layers down in the organization. This kind of communication is directly at odds with the communication policy laid down in the premerger corporation, which emphasized direct-line reporting.

A consequence of this network information process is that we often have to wait for the right time to make a decision. We call the wait a "creative stall." In the old organization it would have been called procrastination, but what we're doing is waiting for some important players to come "on-side" before making an announcement.[9] In our terms, you "prepare in the box and wait in the bubble."

Once the time is right, however, implementation is rapid. Everyone is totally involved and has given thought to what has to be done. Not only is the time it takes for the decision to be made and implemented shorter than in the past but also the whole process strengthens the organization rather than weakening it through bitterness about how the decision was made.

☐ People ...&... ○ People

☐ *Rational*   ○ *Social*

☐ *Produce*   ○ *Create*

☐ *Think*   ○ *Imagine*

☐ *Tell*   ○ *Inspire*

☐ *Work*   ○ *Play*

In the old, premerger days, it was convenient to regard employees as rational, welfare-maximizing beings; it made motivating them so much easier and planning less messy.

But because the crisis made it necessary to close many operations and terminate thousands of employees, we had to deal with people's social nature. We could prepare people intellectually by sharing our opinions and, to some extent, protect them physically with severance packages, but we struggled with how to handle the emotional aspects. Especially for long-service employees, severing the bond with the company was the emotional equivalent of death.

Humor is what rescued us. Laughter allows people to jump out of their emotional boxes, or rigid belief structures. None of us can remember having laughed as much as we have over the past three years. Although much of the humor has inevitably been of the gallows variety, it has been an important ingredient in releasing tension and building trust.

Now everyone knows that people are social as well as rational animals. Indeed, we knew it back in the premerger days, but somehow back then we never came to grips with the social aspect, maybe because the rational view of people has an appealing simplicity and clarity. Lombard's Law applied to us—routine, structured tasks drove out nonroutine, unstructured activities.[10]

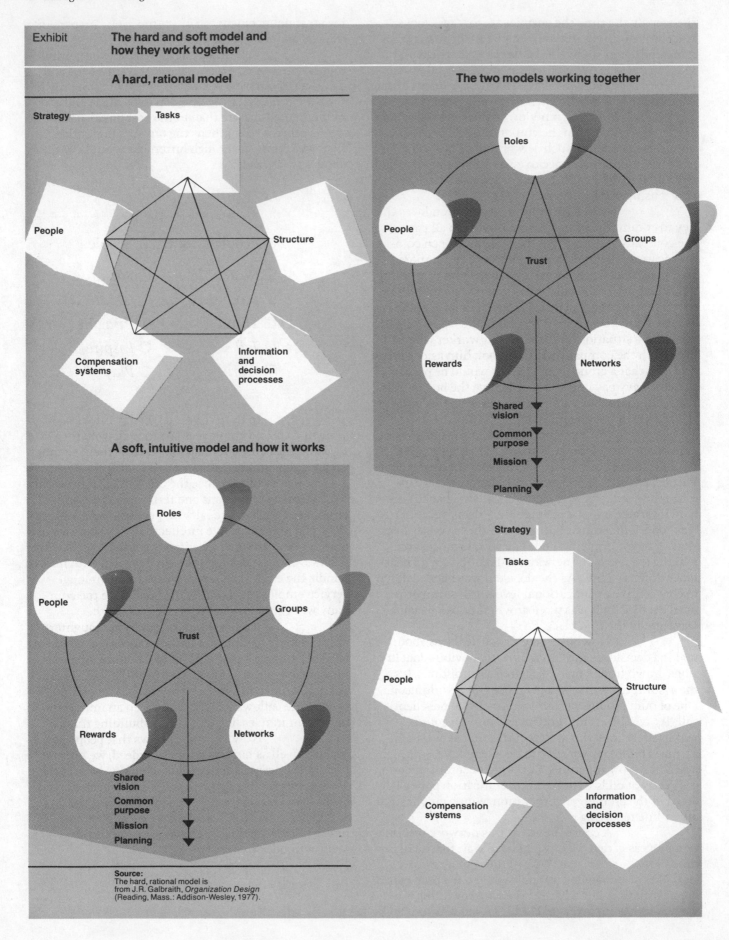

Exhibit   **The hard and soft model and how they work together**

A hard, rational model

Strategy → Tasks

People

Structure

Compensation systems

Information and decision processes

A soft, intuitive model and how it works

Roles

People

Groups

Trust

Rewards

Networks

Shared vision

Common purpose

Mission

Planning

The two models working together

Roles

People

Groups

Trust

Rewards

Networks

Shared vision

Common purpose

Mission

Planning

Strategy

Tasks

People

Structure

Compensation systems

Information and decision processes

Source:
The hard, rational model is
from J.R. Galbraith, *Organization Design*
(Reading, Mass.: Addison-Wesley, 1977).

□ Compensation systems ...&... ○ Rewards

□ Direct	○ Indirect
□ Objective	○ Subjective
□ Profit	○ Fun
□ Failure	○ Mistake
□ Hygiene	○ Motivator
□ Managing	○ Caring

In our premerger organization, the "total compensation policy" meant you could take your money any way you liked—salary, loans, fringes, and so forth. Management thought this policy catered to individual needs and was, therefore, motivating. Similarly, the "Personnel Development Program" required managers to make formal annual reviews of their employees' performances. For some reason, management thought that this also had something to do with motivation. The annual reviews, however, had become a meaningless routine, with managers constrained to be nice to the review subject because they had to work with him or her the next day.

The 1981 recession put a stop to all this by spurring us to freeze all direct compensation. Profit-based compensation disappeared; morale went up.

The management team discussed this decision for hours. As the savings from the freeze would pay for a few weeks' interest only, the numbers made no sense at all. Some of us prophesied doom. "We will lose the best people," we argued. Instead, the symbolic freeze brought the crisis home to everyone. We had all made a sacrifice, a contribution that senior management could recognize at a future time.

Even though the academics say they aren't scientifically valid, we still like Frederick Herzberg's definition of motivators (our interpretations of them are in parentheses):[11]

Achievement (what you believe you did).
Recognition (what others think you did).
Work itself (what you really do).
Responsibility (what you help others do).
Advancement (what you think you can do).
Growth (what you believe you might do).

The new framework at work

The diagram of the soft model in the exhibit shows our view of how our management process seems to work. When the motivating rewards are applied to people playing the necessary roles and working together in groups that are characterized by open communication and are linked to networks throughout the organization, the immediate product is a high degree of mutual trust. This trust allows groups to develop a shared vision that in turn enhances a sense of common purpose. From this process people develop a feeling of having a mission of their own. The mission is spiritual in the sense of being an important effort much larger than oneself. This kind of involvement is highly motivating. Mission is the soft counterpart of strategy.

□ Strategy ...&... ○ Mission

□ Objectives	○ Values
□ Policies	○ Norms
□ Forecast	○ Vision
□ Clockworks	○ Frameworks
□ Right	○ Useful
□ Target	○ Direction
□ Precise	○ Vague
□ Necessary	○ Sufficient

Listed are some of our favorite words for contrasting these two polarities. We find them useful for understanding why clear definition of objectives is not essential for motivating people. Hard box planners advocate the hard box elements and tend to be overinvested in using their various models, or "clockworks" as we call them. Whether it's a Boston Consulting Group matrix or an Arthur D. Little life-cycle curve, too often planners wind them up and managers act according to what they dictate without looking at the assumptions, many of which may be invalid, implicit in the frameworks.

We use the models only as take-off points for discussion. They do not have to be right, only useful. If they don't yield genuine insights we put them aside. The hard box cannot be dispensed with. On the contrary, it is essential—but not sufficient.

The key element in developing a shared purpose is mutual trust. Without trust, people will engage in all kinds of self-centered behavior to assert their own identities and influence coworkers to their own ends. Under these circumstances, they just won't hear others, and efforts to develop a shared vision are doomed. Nothing destroys trust faster than hard box attitudes toward problems that don't require such treatment.

Trust is self-reproductive. When trust is present in a situation, chain reactions occur as people share frameworks and exchange unshielded views. The closer and more tightly knit the group is, the more likely it is that these reactions will spread, generating a shared vision and common purpose.

Once the sense of common purpose and mission is established, the managing group is ready to enter the hard box of strategy (see the right-hand side of the exhibit). Now the specifics of task, structure, information, and decision processes are no longer likely to be controversial or threatening. Implementation becomes astonishingly simple. Action plans are necessary to control hard box implementation, but once the participants in the soft bubble share the picture, things seem to happen by themselves as team members play their roles and fill the gaps as they see them. Since efforts to seize control of bubble activity are likely to prove disastrous, it is most fortunate that people act spontaneously without being "organized." Paradoxically, one can achieve control in the bubble only by letting go—which gets right back to trust.

In the hard box, the leadership model is that of the general who gives crisp, precise instructions as to who is to do what and when. In the soft bubble, the leadership model is that of the shepherd, who follows his flock watchfully as it meanders along the natural contours of the land. He carries the weak and collects the strays, for they all have a contribution to make. This style may be inefficient, but it is effective. The whole flock reaches its destination at more or less the same time.[12]

□ **Boxes** ...&...	○ **Bubbles**
□ Solve	○ Dissolve
□ Sequential	○ Lateral
□ Left brain	○ Right brain
□ Serious	○ Humorous
□ Explain	○ Explore
□ Rational	○ Intuitive
□ Conscious	○ Unconscious
□ Learn	○ Remember .
□ Knowledge	○ Wisdom
□ Lens	○ Mirror
□ Full	○ Empty
□ Words	○ Pictures
□ Objects	○ Symbols
□ Description	○ Parable

Thought and language are keys to changing perceptions. Boxes and bubbles describe the hard and soft thought structures, respectively. Boxes have rigid, opaque sides; walls have to be broken down to join boxes, although if the lid is off one can jump out. Bubbles have flexible, transparent sides that can easily expand and join with other bubbles. Bubbles float but can easily burst. In boxes problems are to be solved; in bubbles they are dissolved. The trick is to change the context of the problem, that is, to jump out of the box. This technique has many applications.

We have noticed a number of articles in your publication that concern values and ethics in business, and some people have suggested that business students be required to attend classes in ethics. From our view of the world, sending students to specific courses is a hard box solution and would be ineffective. Ethical behavior is absent from some businesses not because the managers have no ethics (or have the wrong ones) but because the hard "strategy box" does not emphasize them as being valuable. The hard box deals in objectives, and anyone who raises value issues in that context will not survive long.

In contrast, in the "mission bubble" people feel free to talk about values and ethics because there is trust. The problem of the lack of ethical behavior is dissolved.

We have found bubble thinking to be the intellectual equivalent of judo; a person does not resist an attacker but goes with the flow, thereby adding his strength to the other's momentum. Thus when suppliers demanded that their financial exposure to our lack of creditworthiness be reduced, we agreed and suggested that they protect themselves by supplying goods to us on consignment. After all, their own financial analysis showed we couldn't pay them any money! In some cases we actually got consignment deals, and where we didn't the scheme failed because of nervous lawyers (also hard box players) rather than reluctance on the part of the supplier.

Bubble thought structures are characterized by what Edward de Bono calls lateral thinking.[13] The sequential or vertical thought structure is logical and rational; it proceeds through logical stages and depends on a yes-no test at each step. De Bono suggests that in lateral thinking the yes-no test must be suspended, for the purpose is to explore not explain, to test assumptions not conclusions.

We do the same kind of questioning when we do what we call "humming a lot." When confronted with what initially appears to be an unpalatable idea, an effective manager will say "hmm" and wait until the idea has been developed and its implications considered. Quite often, even when an initial idea is out of the question, the fact that we have considered it seriously will lead to a different, innovative solution.

We have found it useful to think of the action opposite to the one we intend taking. When selling businesses we found it helpful to think about acquiring purchasers. This led to deeper research into purchasers' backgrounds and motives and to a more effective packaging and presentation of the businesses to be sold. This approach encourages novel ideas and makes the people who generate them (the entrepreneurs) feel that their ideas, however "dumb," will not be rejected out of hand.

In hard box thought structures, one tends to use conceptual frameworks as lenses, to sit on one side and examine an object on the other. In bubble structures, the frameworks are mirrors reflecting one's own nature and its effect on one's perceptions; object and subject are on the same side. In the hard box, knowledge is facts, from learning; in the bubble, knowledge is wisdom, from experience.

Bubble thought structures are not easily described in words. Language itself is a box reflecting our cultural heritage and emphasizing some features of reality at the expense of others. Part of our struggle during the past three years has been to unlearn many scientific management concepts and develop a new vocabulary. We have come up with some new phrases and words: management by walking around, creative stall, asking dumb questions, jumping out of the box, creating a crisis, humming a lot, and muddling. We have also attached new meanings to old words such as fact and perception, independence and autonomy, hard and soft, solve and dissolve, and so forth.

Three years later

What we have told you about works in a crisis. And we can well understand your asking whether this approach can work when the business is stable and people lapse back into boxes. We have developed two methods of preventing this lapse.

1   **If there isn't a crisis, we create one.** One way to stir things up is familiar to anyone who has ever worked in a hard box organization. Intimidation, terror, and the use of raw power will produce all the stress you need. But eventually people run out of adrenalin and the organization is drained, not invigorated.

In a bubble organization, managers dig for opportunities in a much more relaxed manner. During the last three years, for instance, many of our divisions that were profitable and liquid were still in need of strategic overhaul. During the course of walking around, we unearthed many important issues by asking dumb questions.

The more important of the issues that surface this way offer an opportunity to put a champion (someone who believes in the importance of the issue) in charge of a team of people who can play all the roles required to handle the issue. The champion then sets out with his or her group to go through the incremental development process—developing trust, building both a hard box picture and a shared vision, and, finally, establishing strategy. By the time the strategy is arrived at, the task force disciples have such zeal and sense of mission that they are ready to take the issue to larger groups, using the same process.

Two by-products of asking dumb questions deserve mention. First, when senior management talks to people at all levels, people at all levels start talking to each other. Second, things tend to get fixed before they break. In answering a senior manager's casual question, a welder on the shop floor of a steel fabrication plant revealed that some critical welds had failed quality tests and the customer's inspector was threatening to reject an entire bridge. A small ad hoc task force, which included the inspector (with the customer's permission), got everyone off the hook and alerted top management to a potential weakness in the quality control function.

Applying the principles in other areas takes years to bear fruit. We are now using the process to listen to customers and suppliers. We never knew how to do this before. Now it is clear that it is necessary to create an excuse (crisis) for going to see them, share "secrets," build trust, share a vision, and capture them in your bubble. It's very simple, and early results have been excellent. We call it a soft revolution.

2   **Infuse activities that some might think prosaic with real significance.** The focus should be on people first, and always on caring rather than managing. The following approach works in good times as well as bad:

> Use a graphic vocabulary that describes what you do.

> Share confidential information, personal hopes and fears to create a common vision and promote trust.

> Seize every opportunity (open doors, management by walking around, networks) to make a point, emphasize a value, disseminate information, share an experience, express interest, and show you care.

> Recognize performance and contribution of as many people as possible. Rituals and ceremonies—retirements, promotions, birthdays—present great opportunities.

> Use incentive programs whose main objective is not compensation but recognition.

We have tried to approach things this way, and for us the results have been significant. Now, three years after the crisis first struck our corporation, we are a very different organization. Of our 25 divisions, we have closed 7 and sold 16. Five of the latter were bought by Federal Industries, Ltd. of Winnipeg. Some 860 employees including us, the four members of the management team, have gone to Federal. These divisions are healthy and raring to go. Two divisions remain at York Russel, which has changed its name to YRI-YORK, Ltd.

Now we face new questions, such as how one recruits into a management team. We know that we have to help people grow into the team, and fortunately we find that they flourish in our warm climate. But trust takes time to develop, and the bubble is fragile. The risk is greatest when we have to transplant a senior person from outside, because time pressures may not allow us to be sure we are compatible. The danger is not only to the team itself but also to the person joining it.

Our new framework has given us a much deeper appreciation of the management process and the roles effective general managers play. For example, it is clear that while managers can delegate tasks in the hard box rather easily—perhaps because they can define them—it's impossible to delegate soft bubble activities. The latter are difficult to isolate from each other because their integration takes place in one brain.

Similarly, the hard box general management roles of producer and administrator can be formally taught, and business schools do a fine job of it. The soft roles of entrepreneur and integrator can probably not be taught formally. Instead, managers must learn from mentors. Over time they will adopt behavior patterns that allow them to play the required roles. It would seem, however, that natural ability and an individual's upbringing probably play a much larger part in determining effectiveness in the soft roles than in the hard roles; it is easier to teach a soft bubble player the hard box roles than it is to teach the soft roles to a hard box player.

In the three-year period when we had to do things so differently, we created our own culture, with its own language, symbols, norms, and customs. As with other groups, the acculturation process began when people got together in groups and trusted and cared about each other.[14]

In contrast with our premerger culture, the new culture is much more sympathetic toward and supportive of the use of teams and consensus decision making. In this respect, it would seem to be similar to oriental ways of thinking that place a premium on the same processes. Taoists, for instance, would have no trouble recognizing the polarities of the hard box and the soft bubble and the need to keep a balance between the two.[15]

□ Heaven ...&... ○ Earth

□ Yang	○ Yin
□ Father	○ Mother
□ Man	○ Woman

These symbols are instructive. After all, most of us grew up with two bosses: father usually played the hard box parts, while mother played the soft, intuitive, and entrepreneurial roles. The family is the original team, formed to handle the most complex management task ever faced. Of late, we seem to have fired too many of its members—a mistake we can learn from.

Toward a managerial theory of relativity

The traditional hard box view of management, like the traditional orientation of physics, is valid (and very useful) only within a narrow range of phenomena. Once one gets outside the range, one needs new principles. In physics, cosmologists at the macro level as well as students of subatomic particles at the micro level use Einstein's theory of relativity as an explanatory principle and set Newton's physics aside.[16] For us, the theory in the bubble is our managerial theory of relativity. At the macro level it reminds us that how management phenomena appear depends on one's perspective and biases. At the micro level we remember that all jobs have both hard and soft components.

This latter point is of particular importance to people like us in the service industry. The steel we distribute is indistinguishable from anyone else's. We insist on rigid standards regarding how steel is handled, what reporting systems are used, and so forth. But hard box standards alone wouldn't be enough to set us apart from our competitors. That takes service, a soft concept. And everyone has to be involved. Switchboard operators are in the front line; every contact is an opportunity to share the bubble. Truck drivers and warehouse workers make their own special contribution—by taking pride in the cleanliness of their equipment or by keeping the inventory neat and accessible.

With the box and bubble concept, managers can unlock many of the paradoxes of management and handle the inherent ambiguities. You don't do one or the other absolutely; you do what is appropriate. For instance, the other day in one of our operations the biweekly payroll run deducted what appeared to be random amounts from the sales representatives' pay packets. The branch affected was in an uproar. After taking some hard box steps to remedy the situation, our vice president of human resources seized the opportunity to go out to the branch and talk to the sales team. He was delighted with the response. The sales force saw that he understood the situation and cared about them, and he got to meet them all, which will make future contacts easier. But neither the hard box nor soft bubble approach on its own would have been appropriate. We need both. As one team member put it, "You have to find the bubble in the box and put the box in the bubble." Exactly.

The amazing thing is that the process works so well. The spirit of cooperation among senior managers is intense, and we seem to be getting "luckier" as we go along. When a "magic" event takes place it means that somehow we got the timing just right.[17] And there is great joy in that.

References

1 Thomas J. Peters and Robert H. Waterman, *In Search of Excellence* (New York: Harper and Row, 1982), p. 29.

2 For the best of the hard box models we have come across, see Jay R. Galbraith, *Organization Design* (Reading, Mass.: Addison-Wesley, 1977).

3 Henry Mintzberg, "The Manager's Job: Folklore and Fact," HBR July-August 1975, p. 49.

4 Edgar H. Schein, *Process Consultation: Its Role in Organization Development* (Reading, Mass.: Addison-Wesley, 1969).

5 Ichak Adize, *How to Solve the Mismanagement Crisis* (Los Angeles: MDOR Institute, 1979).

6 Edgar H. Schein's *Process Consultation*, p. 10, was very helpful in showing us how the process differs from the content.

7 Getting consensus among a group of managers poses the same challenge as negotiating a deal. *Getting to Yes* by Robert Fisher and William Ury (Boston: Houghton Mifflin, 1981) is a most helpful book for understanding the process.

8 For discussion of the importance of networks, see John P. Kotter, "What Effective General Managers Really Do," HBR November-December 1982, p. 156.

9 For discussion of a "creative stall" being applied in practice, see Stratford P. Sherman, "Muddling to Victory at Geico," *Fortune*, September 5, 1983, p. 66.

10 Louis B. Barnes, "Managing the Paradox of Organizational Trust," HBR March-April 1981, p. 107.

11 In "One More Time: How Do You Motivate Employees?" HBR January-February 1968, p. 53.

12 For another view of the shepherd role, see the poem by Nancy Esposito, "The Good Shepherd," HBR July-August 1983, p. 121.

13 See Edward de Bono, *The Use of Lateral Thinking* (London: Jonathan Cape, 1967), and *PO: Beyond Yes and No* (New York: Simon and Schuster, 1972).

14 To explore the current concern with creating strong organizational cultures in North American corporations, see Terrence E. Deal and Alan A. Kennedy *Corporate Cultures* (Reading, Mass.: Addison-Wesley, 1982).

15 For discussion of Tao and some applications, we highly recommend Benjamin Hoff, *The Tao of Pooh* (New York: E.P. Dutton, 1982), p. 67; also Allen Watts, *Tao: The Watercourse Way* (New York: Pantheon Books, 1975).

16 Fritjof Capra, *The Tao of Physics* (London: Fontana Paperbacks, 1983).

17 Carl Jung developed the concept of synchronicity to explain such events. See, for example, Ira Progoff, *Jung, Synchronicity and Human Destiny—Non-Causal Dimensions of Human Experience* (New York: Julian Press, 1973). For an excellent discussion of Jung's work and its relevance to our times, see Laurens van de Post, *Jung and the Story of Our Time* (New York: Random House, 1975).

Managing technological change: a box of cigars for Brad

The CEO of Diversified Manufacturing Corporation learns a lesson about top management's role in overseeing technological advance in product lines

Frederick W. Gluck and Richard N. Foster

Brad Youngman, brash young vice president for corporate development at Diversified Manufacturing Corporation, handed his boss, Miles Atkinson, a lengthy memo just as the CEO was about to board a jet for a welcome vacation in Jamaica. The memo from the trouble-shooter essentially asked, "Who the hell is running this business?" Youngman's analysis of what constitutes the strategic direction of a technology-based company leads to a reexamination by Atkinson and his top management group of their roles in the operation of the company. The lesson that Atkinson learns is a valuable one for any high executive.

Frederick W. Gluck and Richard N. Foster are principal and associate, respectively, in the New York City office of McKinsey & Company, the consulting firm. The authors have a special interest in the problems of technology-based companies.

I don't think I've ever been so glad to get on an airplane in my life, thought Miles. *Another 15 minutes with Brad and I probably would have fired him.*

Miles Atkinson settled into his seat on the 747 flight to Jamaica. He was on his way to join his wife, Moira, at their villa in Montego Bay for their first real vacation since he had become president and chief executive of Diversified Manufacturing Corporation five years before. It had been a tremendous but demanding five years for the manufacturer of construction, medical, and (now) oil-drilling equipment: sales up 120%, profits up 80%, some successes, and some failures. Moira had really been after him lately. She said he had begun to stew about his problems and needed a rest.

She's probably right, he thought. *Look at how frustrated I am with Brad. But goddamn it, I know he's a good man.*

The immediate cause of his frustration was the lunch he'd just had with Bradford Youngman, his vice president for corporate development. Brad was a real tiger. DMC had picked him up three years before when it acquired Dynamic Controls, a small, high-technology company that Brad and two partners had built from scratch. Six months ago Miles had persuaded Brad to leave the subsidiary, which was clearly too small to test him rigorously, and give him a hand with strategy at corporate headquarters.

Miles admitted to himself that he didn't have quite the same handle on the business that he'd had five years before when he'd stepped up from executive VP of manufacturing to the presidency. So he wanted Brad to develop a corporate planning system

Exhibit I
Miles Atkinson's activity profile

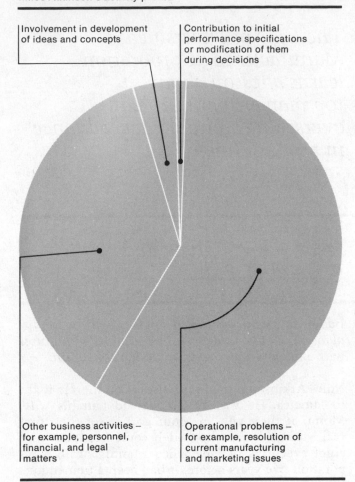

Involvement in development of ideas and concepts

Contribution to initial performance specifications or modification of them during decisions

Other business activities – for example, personnel, financial, and legal matters

Operational problems – for example, resolution of current manufacturing and marketing issues

that would pull things together and help him set a clear strategic direction for Diversified. It had been quite a struggle persuading Brad that the move made sense for him.

Now, ironically, the question was whether it had made sense for the company—Brad was turning out to be bad news. Instead of working on a planning system, he was minding everybody else's business. In particular, he was constantly second-guessing the technical people on technical decisions. Cutler Sims, VP for finance, and Jim Pasinaro, VP for R&D, were livid over Brad's nit-picking at one of the most sophisticated R&D project evaluation systems in the industry. And two hours ago at lunch Brad had implied none too subtly that top management—that is, Miles himself—wasn't providing the leadership that DMC needed. To top it off, Brad had dropped another of his memos on Miles and insisted that he take it along on his vacation.

Could the guy possibly have his eye on my job? thought Miles. *If he does, he's sure telegraphing his punches. Well, the hell with him and his memo. I'll look at it later.*

Two weeks later, on the flight back to New York, Miles reflected that Moira had been right again. *I really needed that vacation; I was getting paranoid. Imagine seeing a threat in Brad's criticism. Why, the guy was only—oh, Lord, that memo of his. I'd better look at it or he'll be all over me.*

Shaking up the CEO

MEMORANDUM

TO:
Miles Atkinson,
President,
Diversified Manufac-
turing Corporation

FROM:
Bradford Youngman,
Vice President,
Corporate Development

It's been six months since you sweet-talked me into this boondoggle at headquarters, and I'll bet you're sitting there at 35,000 feet wondering whether it was the right thing to do. I know I've been a royal pain you know where, and some people think I've been sticking my nose in places where it doesn't belong. Well, if these six months have been difficult for you, they haven't been exactly comfortable for me. But I think all the snooping I've done may turn out to be worthwhile.

To get at the substance of our problems, as you asked me to do, I had to dig into the business. Since we're a technology-based company, that meant digging into the technology, and specifically into our key product and process design decisions. If I learned one thing at Dynamic, it's that a superior product line and superior cost structure are one hell of a leg up in the marketplace. And in technology-based businesses like Dynamic and Diversified, the only way to get those advantages in the long run is by effectively managing technological advances in the product lines—a very different thing from calculating possible returns from R&D. In fact, the more I dug and the more I thought about it, the more I realized that the way we manage techno-

Exhibit II
Miles's time allocation, showing his ability to influence strategy

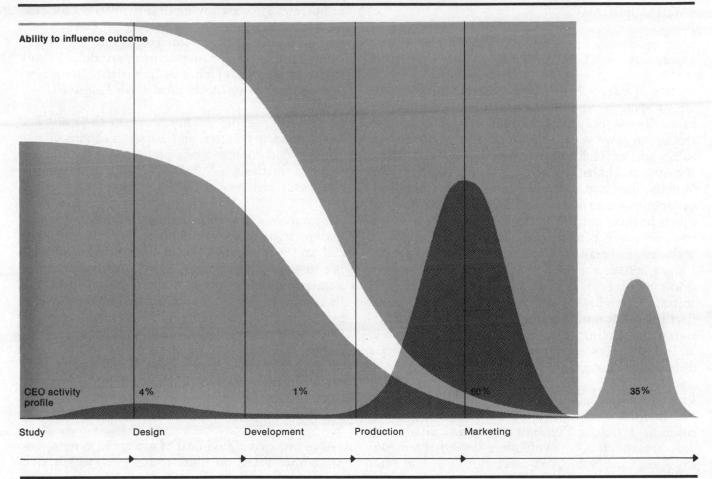

Ability to influence outcome

CEO activity
profile

Study	Design	Development	Production	Marketing
	4%	1%	60%	35%

logical development is the heart of our whole strategic planning. You could call it the "strategic control of technology."

Nice phrase, thought Miles. *So what else is new?*

Once I'd gotten that far, things really began to fall into place. It was obvious that the leverage to influence the outcome of a product design is way up front—not months before you go into production, but even before you start the design. We're damned effective at manufacturing cost reduction, but if we're cost-reducing a design that's inherently more expensive than a competitor's, we're playing catch-up ball. And I don't have to tell you that if the design misses the market or challenges the regulations, we're really in the soup.

Touché. We spent a small fortune on dust-proofing those ore conveyors after we put them on the market.

By the way, Miles, do you recall the last time you had a hand in deciding the performance characteristics of a new design, or really understood why we needed it? I went through your appointment books for last year—the ones you asked me to look at to become familiar with your modus operandi. Take a look at the first chart that I prepared [see *Exhibit I*]. You spend, at most, 5% of your time on the substance of the major product and process decisions that not only establish our technological strategy but also largely define our business strategy. Fire fighting and other operating problems take up 60% of your time, and you devote 35% to legal, financial, personnel, and other matters.

In the second chart that I made [*Exhibit II*], I've applied your time profile to a diagram showing how our flexibility to set the strategic direction of DMC decreases as an idea moves through concept and design and into the marketplace. It looks like you're apportioning your time in roughly inverse relation to the strategic importance of each phase. This suggests a rather basic question: Who the hell is running the business?

Brad, old buddy, thought Miles grimly, *if you don't know, rest easy. You'll find out.*

As I mentioned before, we're intervening in the wrong spots. At the top level of the company we're primarily exercising operational, not strategic, control because we've become so far removed from the substance of technological decisions. Sure, that's the nuts and bolts, in a sense; but in a company like ours the nuts and bolts *are* strategy. The technological options are so diverse and the market needs are so much in flux that the strategic performance parameters of every product and line—the features that make us or break us—are constantly shifting. And I don't believe that you or anyone else at the decision-making level is systematically analyzing these shifts and modifying our technical strategies to reflect them. Most of the time we're content to rubber-stamp the technical guys' decisions quite a while after design gets under way and when the strategic direction has long since been cast in concrete.

Rubber-stamp, hell. I go over those things with a fine-toothed comb. Sure, maybe the R&D reviews could be advanced a bit, but it wouldn't change the outcome much. Our evaluation system weeds out the losers long before they reach me. Or is that what he's driving at?

Five years ago, when you were made CEO, I'll bet you could have told me the important design parameters of every one of our major products and exactly why they were the way they were. But can you tell me now why we still have electromechanical controls on our heavy earthmovers? That's not an idle question, Miles. Five years ago our controls for this equipment were the best and most reliable on the market, and everyone knew it. That gave us a clean competitive edge. On top of that, over the years we'd cost-reduced them to the point where we could price them very competitively and still throw off loads of cash. But over the past five years, as you know, our edge has been eroding as our competitors put solid-state devices into their controls.

And next fall, of course, Focused Industries is introducing integrated circuits on all its heavy equipment control systems. Meanwhile, our study team is still trying to decide which supplier to work with. Pasinaro says our electromechanical systems have done the trick for seven years and the new ones

still have some bugs in them. I've looked into it and I'm not persuaded. Meanwhile, Sid Rogers and half of his sales guys are saying that the market for electromechanical controls will dry up so fast it won't be funny once FI's new line comes out. Personally, I don't think Sid is just preparing an alibi; I think there's a very good chance he's right. Remember what happened to Mechanical Cash Register?

I remember, all right. They stuck to their last and kept producing better and better mechanical machines while their competitors went electronic—and mopped up the floor with MCR. But hell, calculators aren't earthmovers.

For somebody in your position, there's a natural but extremely dangerous temptation to focus on financial and mathematical abstractions instead of coming to grips with the realities of our business economics and competitive product-line position. The literature is full of sophisticated analytical and mathematical procedures for R&D management: DCF analysis, project-ranking procedures, experience curves, nonlinear programming for project selection under uncertainty, multidimensional scaling techniques for determining desirable product characteristics, industrial dynamics simulations of entire companies, and so on, ad infinitum.

We've invested a good deal of money in systems and procedures based on these techniques, which gives us a comfortable feeling that we've reduced our problems to hard, reliable figures. So we don't worry nearly as much as we should about all those subtle, elusive, qualitative factors that the figures don't reflect. We forget that our job as top managers is to manage product lines, not financial abstractions. Sure, we need to reduce a lot of data to sophisticated digests, but to do the job we're paid for we also need plenty of unabstracted information, with all the fuzziness of reality in it.

There's no substitute for fact-founded judgment on technological issues. And while these techniques and the financial analyses are useful and have their place, they simply don't tell the whole story. That's the nature of the beast.

Agreed, Brad, agreed—you can't have too much information. But where am I supposed to get the time to dig down to that level of detail? Who's going to mind the store?

I think we've lost strategic control of the company because we've let a group of guys about three levels below Pasinaro make our basic technical and business decisions. And they don't have the perspective needed to handle them. We hardly ever tell *them* what to do; they tell *us* what they're doing. At the most, we judge whether what they've got in the works will fly in the marketplace. We've become overdependent on management by exception, but I doubt we're even very effective at that. When was the last time, Miles, that you shut off a project as a result of an R&D review?

Maybe four years ago. Well, not shut off exactly; I didn't approve the A-300 until they'd redesigned it to a higher level of maintainability.

Look at the way we've been depending on the R&D people and the marketing people to set priorities for our technology. Most of the time we haven't even defined the missions to be accomplished, except in financial terms. Sometimes, when it comes to reviewing our alternatives, we pass the buck to a committee or task force. Nine times out of ten they follow some variation of the Chinese menu approach. You get three options—Option A boils down to doing nothing, Option B is radical and terrifyingly risky, and Option C is a nice, safe, well-balanced compromise with something for everybody, backed up with lots of reassuring analysis. And you get to sprinkle holy water.

Meanwhile, up in the corporate stratosphere, we've allowed ourselves to become insulated from the technological realities—when to shift from electromechanical to solid-state, say, or from discrete components to integrated circuits. And we've even become insulated from some of the market realities—when to try to segment a market by creating unique performance specs, as you did with the Model A-300. We even fumble over developing control systems that will meet new EPA and OSHA regulations. We let the lawyers and the R&D staff worry about the problem.

In general, we're allowing big technological decisions to be made by some very bright people who are at such a low level in the organization that they can't see the trees for the undergrowth, let alone the forest for the trees. Subtle but critical trade-offs involving manufacturing cost, product features, reliability, and date of introduction are made almost daily at the design level. We could be missing a major market opportunity or crippling our economics just because a single designer or his boss would rather walk over his grandmother than exceed his budget.

That may have been MCR's problem—maybe it could be traced to the company's brittle financial control, everyone frightened of spending a dollar, no one rocking the boat. How many millions has MCR written off now?

Well, Miles, this memo has gone on longer than I intended, and I'm going to cut it off. Before doing so, however, I want to say two more things.

First, I don't believe our situation is all that bleak yet. I've talked to people in a lot of other companies about these problems, and most of them, outside of the really top performers, seem to be muddling along pretty much the way we are. And we *have* made quite a few good decisions. But we owe half of them to luck or dumb decisions by our competitors, which I guess is much the same thing. We can thank our stars that the quality of our people has partly compensated for our failure to manage technological change. On the other hand, we've always been the industry leader, and we don't want to let that slip away from us.

Second, I want to ask you to take the attached list of questions to the annual R&D budget review meeting the Tuesday after you get back from Montego Bay. If you see fit, ask a few of the questions then. I'm going to be uncharacteristically quiet.

Well, Miles, I hope I haven't given you indigestion. See you on Tuesday.

Probing questions

Thoroughly aroused by Brad's comments, Miles pored over the list. He added a couple of questions to it, rearranged the order of the questions, and wrote out a final list, as follows:

Finance
(Cutler Sims)

1
How many R&D projects have been proposed to top management in the past five years? How many has it turned down or substantially modified?
2
Of the projects we have approved, what was the distribution of projected rates of return?

R&D and Sales
(Jim Pasinaro, Sid Rogers)

1
How do our present electromechanical control systems stack up against Focused Industries' line in terms of technology, reliability, maintenance, and cost structure?
2
How will Focused's new integrated-circuit line affect us? What do we plan to do in response?
3
What do our customers regard as the three most important performance parameters of our control systems in earthmoving equipment? In medical equipment? In oil-drilling equipment?
4
How do we stack up against Focused in each of these markets in terms of these parameters?
5
Are there any anticipated changes in external developments—e.g., legislative or regulatory action or shifts in raw material availability—that could change the strategic performance parameters of our products in these markets?
6
How do our R&D programs reflect these considerations? How much technological risk are we taking in introducing the new drilling-equipment line? How much marketing risk?

Back at his desk at 9 a.m. Monday, Miles dictated three brief memoranda, one to each of the three VPs, listing the relevant questions and requesting each man to bring the answers with him to the review the next day. Then he shut himself up for the rest of the day and dealt with two weeks' accumulation of paper.

Confrontation on Tuesday

Reviews of the budget, of the ratios of R&D expense to sales, and of the other customary financial gauges of the R&D effort took up the first part of the meeting. Pasinaro had just finished with the chart summarizing new-project ROIs and was about to start the project-by-project ROI reviews when Miles asked the finance VP his first question: "Cutler, your finance guys track our project selection system pretty closely. What percent of the projects that are proposed to us have been turned down since we started this process?"

"Well, Miles," said Cutler, "I'd never really looked at that before, but I followed it up for you. It looks as if we'd never actually turned a project down. Once they get to us, it's pretty automatic because the losers have already been screened out. I'd say that's as it should be."

Score one for Brad, thought Miles. *He said that's what they'd say.* "I see," he said. "And what about the distribution of projected rates of return?"

"I have that one too," said Cutler. "Of course, given that we've never turned a project down, no projection has fallen below the 20% hurdle rate. But I was a little surprised to find that 95% of the projections over the past three years, since we got the system on line, have come in between 20% and 25%. It's possible that some of the boys down the line have been plugging numbers. You know how hard it is to project sales from new products."

"Yes, I know." *"Possible," my foot; it's a dead certainty, and he knows it.* "Jim," said Miles, turning to Pasinaro, "I know we have high hopes for those new drilling-equipment controls. If that line succeeds, it will have a major impact on next year's earnings. How much technical risk are we taking in that project?"

"Miles, I'm happy to report that there's nothing to worry about there. The system is a classic design, and there isn't a component in it that hasn't been proved out over time in our electromechanical devices. The whole project is solid as a rock, technically. Being conservative," Pasinaro concluded, "I'll say it's 99% risk free."

That's great, Miles thought wryly. *You'll guarantee the product will work if anyone happens to buy it.* "Jim," he continued, "what features of our control systems are most important to potential customers in this market, and how will the program help our market position relative to, say, Focused Industries?"

"I'm not sure I follow you, Miles. We've never looked at it in quite that way. Our customers want four main things—low cost, high performance, low maintenance, and high reliability. We're tops in every single one of these counts, and we aim to stay that way."

"Staying tops in market share is what I had in mind," Miles said dryly. "Thanks anyway, Jim. Sid, how would you estimate the marketing risk in this introduction?"

"Well, you know how hard it is to estimate sales of new products," Rogers said. "I hate to commit myself, but we've got a solid cadre of loyal customers in that market segment, and we're going to hold them and add to them with this new line. Cutler, you've got the charts. What are we projecting that market as?"

Miles interrupted him. "No, Sid, I know we've got the projections. I want to know about the risk. What's the chance that the projections won't materialize?"

"I hope I don't seem to be ducking the question, Miles, but we haven't really looked at it that way. How the hell could we calculate that risk? To be honest, a number of my salesmen are getting kind of nervous about Focused Industries' all solid-state approach. You know salesmen—always crying wolf. Anyway, our headquarters guys have ironed this all out with Jim's people."

"They sure have, Sid." Pasinaro chimed in. "Your guys have extrapolated the market based on some very sophisticated smoothing techniques, and my guys have nailed down the cost and reliability to a gnat's eyeball. I don't see how we can miss."

This is unreal, thought Miles. But before he could speak, Seymour Crawford, the general counsel, interrupted. Miles was rather surprised; Seymour had never been known to say a word at an R&D budget meeting. Usually he had to be coaxed into attending.

"Jim, Sidney," Crawford said, "pardon me for butting in. I just wanted to make sure you're aware of the possibility of some new OSHA legislation prohibiting the use of electromechanical relay contacts on drilling equipment. It's not a certainty this year by any means, but I think the handwriting's on the wall. My assistant, Hal Masterson, took it up with one of your engineers a few weeks ago and got roughly nowhere. Your guy's position, as I heard it, was that our electromechanical devices had the best safety record in the business and that anyway we had no alternative, since we don't make semiconductors. Hal thought that was rather beside the point, but your guy's back was up so he didn't pursue it at the time. I thought you ought to know the story. Mind you, I'm not pushing the panic button."

Horace Bender, the manufacturing VP, spoke up for the first time: "Let's not forget all that electromechanical capacity we just put in, Jim."

"That's right," said Pasinaro. "We're already committed, and, anyway, I think OSHA's a paper tiger."

"I don't know, Jim," Crawford said. "They've been taking some tough stands lately, and the courts have been backing them up. Still, we're probably OK for a while."

They could swat us like a gnat, eyeballs and all, Miles thought.

"Come to think of it," said Rogers, "one of my guys was going on about OSHA last week too. Maybe we should check our contacts in Washington."

They'll have to treat me for depression when this is over. Glancing around the table, Miles saw Cutler, so cool and confident a moment ago, now looking decidedly ill at ease; Sid was pensive; and Seymour was rather above it all. Only Jim and Horace seemed relaxed. Brad was quietly watchful.

As Miles was about to put his next question, Jim Pasinaro took the floor again. "Miles, we're falling way behind schedule with this speculation. I know our guys have studied all these things, and they're satisfied. Now, if you want to finish reviewing the numbers, we'd better get back on track."

"OK, Jim. But before we go on, I'd like to ask you to elaborate a bit on my point about performance parameters. What do you think are the most important features to our customers in the drilling segment, and how will the project under consideration help our competitive position in those areas?"

"Miles, as I said before: cost, reliability, maintainability, performance. That's what all our customers want. Now, if you want details on what our competitors' equipment is like, we've got the complete literature and specs on every one of them in our files. One of our guys can dig them out and answer any questions you might have by the end of the week. But it seems to me that here and now we ought to be concerned with approving our own projects instead of sitting around speculating about a competitor's product line.

"As far as the solid-state issue is concerned, you'll recall that we had a task force look at it two years ago. They concluded that solid-state controls wouldn't take over the market for six to ten years, so we could afford to relax. Or, if we wanted to push it, we could retread half of our engineering staff, hire a bunch of high-priced, solid-state hotshots, and scoop the industry. Nobody was very keen on that one, you remember. What did make sense was to go ahead with our proven electromechanical technology, watch the trends in semiconductors, and review the bidding in two years' time. That's next spring, I reckon."

Now Sims spoke up. "It seems to me, Jim, that we may have let our decision making in these areas get a little too routine. Your down-the-line engineers seem to be making an awful lot of key decisions."

"I don't see anything wrong with that," Pasinaro retorted. "That's exactly what—" whereupon Sid interrupted angrily, and others joined in the hub-bub. But in a few minutes Miles had restored order, and the group completed the agenda as planned.

Then Miles took the floor. "Gentlemen," he said, "it's now past one o'clock. Although personally I seem to have lost my appetite, I suggest we move over to the dining room for lunch. There's no sense in coming back here afterwards, however. It seems clear to me, based on this morning's rather depressing performance, that we're superbly prepared to discuss things of little importance and totally at sea when it comes to assessing the strategic significance of our R&D programs. Obviously, we've all got some hard thinking to do about our approach to managing technological change.

"Since we've never turned down an R&D project before, let's consider this year's R&D budget approved as proposed for the moment and spend the afternoon reflecting on why we seem to be so distant from the realities of our businesses. You'll all be getting a memo on the subject from me early next week."

Shape of a solution

MEMORANDUM

TO:
R&D Planning
Committee

FROM:
Miles Atkinson,
President

I've had a few days to reflect on our meeting last Tuesday and discuss its implications with each of you, so now I want to share my thoughts with you. We agree that we have a serious problem with our approach to managing technological change. We can deal with that problem if we avoid defensiveness, figure out precisely what needs to be done, and do it.

Fortunately, our company is still the leader in its industry, our financial position is sound, and our basic functional skills and technical capabilities are adequate—apart from a few weak spots. So we have the time to analyze and deliberate; but we must also be decisive.

Let me give you some insight into the nature and extent of the problem. Brad, Jim, and Sid have collaborated on a quick-and-dirty analysis that puts it into perspective. In 1970, our competitive position looked roughly like this:

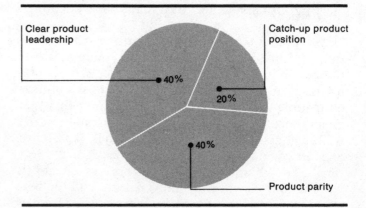

These are the percentages for particular product items in our line, weighted by sales. Today we estimate our competitive position to be as follows:

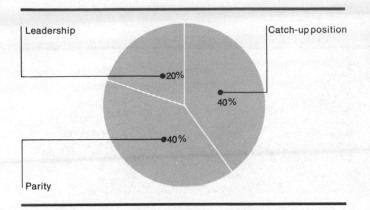

When Focused introduces its new line, it could go to this extreme:

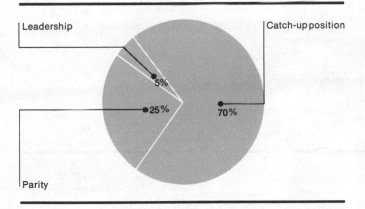

Brad, Sid, and Jim feel that this analysis needs further refining, but that the trend is disturbingly clear. We are steadily losing our competitive position. We haven't felt it too badly yet because we are so well established in our markets, with an extremely loyal customer base. Nevertheless, the trend helps to explain why our sales have gone up half again as fast as our profits over the past five years. And it strongly suggests to me that we've lost our ability to manage technological change effectively.

By now all of you have read and discussed with me Brad's original memo on the subject. We agree that it's an incisive analysis of this insidious loss of strategic control. We've been working so hard to capitalize on our traditional strengths that we've forgotten to look at the strategic performance parameters of our product lines and markets. We've become the captives of tradition and the slaves of procedures. In particular, I have noted the following.

Item: Instead of monitoring the constant changes in technology and in our markets, and modifying our

strategy to maintain our leadership, we have followed the incremental approach that has worked so well in the past—giving our customers more and better of our established products.

Item: We have never tried to balance technological risks and marketing risks. As a result, it appears that our overconservative approach to technological risk is exposing us to a dangerous level of marketing risk.

In short, we simply haven't learned to adapt to change. Let me assure you, I take the largest share of responsibility for the state of affairs that I've just described. But let me also assure you that all of us will have to change our ways radically, starting now. Here are the two main changes we will make:

1   A new kind of review

As top managers, we will participate much earlier in the R&D project selection process; when we do, we will be prepared to make substantive contributions. To this end we will institute monthly, full-day competitive product position reviews, starting one month from today. At these sessions, Sid's marketing people will take the lead in providing an in-depth analysis of one of our major product lines and/or market segments. These analyses will be circulated to each of us in hard copy a week before the meeting so that we can prepare to deal with the questions they raise. Their contents will consider, at a minimum:

☐
The strategic performance parameters of our products in each product/market segment, how they have shifted over the past five years, and how we can expect them to shift in the next five.
☐
Our position in each parameter compared with that of our principal competitors.
☐
The improvements that our customers would value most in each such parameter.
☐
The changes in each parameter that could lead to either further market segmentation or reaggregation of the market at a level giving us a competitive advantage.
☐
Potential moves of competitors that might undermine our company's advantages in each parameter.

Exhibit III
Top management's monitoring of project

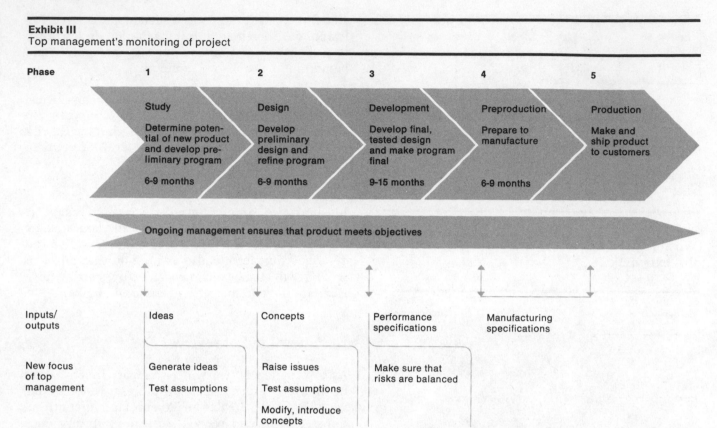

Potential changes in the environment (government action, activity of consumer groups, availability of raw materials) that could weaken our position in, or require changes in, each parameter.

Any other internal or external factor that might make such an impact.

At these sessions we will also evaluate every effort under way to improve each strategic performance parameter, and we will assess these efforts against those of competitors and potential competitors. Jim will report to us on the status of each project and, if possible, of competitive efforts. Supporting the description of each parameter will be a qualitative and, where possible, quantitative estimate of its susceptibility to further modifications through technology. In addition, we will try to pinpoint opportunities for further segmentation or for aggregation of the markets where this strategic factor is relevant.

Note that these reviews will necessarily include some financial analyses. But their focus will be to provide the judgmental raw material required by

our top management group to deal effectively with strategic technological issues.

When we start these reviews, we will naturally have some growing pains. Our first sessions may be uneven. But they should rapidly improve, particularly if we discipline ourselves to record the strategic issues that emerge in these sessions and follow them up to see that they are resolved. I've asked Brad to take responsibility for that follow-up.

These monthly sessions will continue until we have reviewed our entire product line and have identified and understood all the major strategic issues in each of our businesses. At that time we will reassess this new approach and modify it as necessary. Our goal is to develop an exact understanding of what we are doing in R&D, and why.

2 A new boldness in intervention

We will adopt a much more disciplined approach to monitoring the progress of R&D projects. Brad and Jim are still researching the details, but we have already come to a decision on some major requirements.

Henceforth, our new-product introduction process will be divided into discrete phases, as shown in the attached chart [see *Exhibit III*]. Of course, we do this now to a certain extent, but God knows we lack discipline. From now on, before any major project can move from one phase to the next, our top-management group will sign it off. At each sign-off point, we will agree on whether to continue the project and, if we decide to continue it, whether and how the project plan should be modified in the light of new conditions.

I fully expect that this procedure will result in some cancelled projects and substantial redirections of projects as they develop, as we gain better information on technological possibilities and difficulties and, increasingly, as we attune ourselves to developments and changes in the marketplace. This, of course, will differ sharply from our past practice of leaving product development in the hands of R&D once a project had been initially approved and subjecting it to only the most cursory review at our annual budget meetings.

Further, before each sign-off, we will review the competitive position of the product to make sure that the technological and marketing risks remain in balance. We will be less concerned with minimizing schedule delays and cost overruns than with capturing every significant opportunity to strengthen our competitive position through improvements in product performance.

In contrast to our future role, let me note a fact that Cutler has unearthed: with one minor exception, every development project we have undertaken over at least the past five years has been completed with essentially no revision to the original performance specifications, even though substantial shifts in market, competitive, and governmental conditions have taken place. This must never be allowed to happen again. It won't happen if we apply the informed judgment in these matters for which our stockholders are paying us.

Beyond these immediate steps, I am contemplating further moves to streamline our decision making and pinpoint responsibilities for individual businesses and product lines. Since these moves are not yet formed in my mind, I would appreciate suggestions about them from each of you. In the meantime, I know you will cooperate in the fullest with me and also with Brad, as we move to seize strategic control of our technology.

Decisions at the top

Miles breathed a sigh of relief as he shut off his dictating machine. *I deserve one of those Macanudos I brought back from Jamaica*, he thought. *Sara's gone for the day, and she'll never notice that I've been smoking if I remember to clean out the ashtray. I think we're on the way to solving this problem.*

He was feeling pleased with himself. But as the first puffs of his cigar created a gray halo of smoke over his head, he reflected that he was still troubled about the tone of the corporation and the attitudes that underlay the problems he was now moving to solve. If the tone and attitudes were wrong, it was up to him as CEO to change them. He was not yet sure how, but he was beginning to get a handle on the problem.

He had begun with a simple question: What types of technological decisions should his top management team make? The more he thought about it, the more convinced he became that three decisions were key to managing technological change. And as long as DMC was organized as a single profit center, ensuring the soundness of those decisions was his responsibility.

The first was the decision on what to do—that is, what problems or opportunities to deploy technological resources against. Most of the raw material for this decision would have to come from his top functional people during the review sessions. But he would have to immerse himself sufficiently in the issues to be able to ask the right questions and test the assumptions underlying the answers he got. And ultimately he would have to provide direction with respect to the product parameters that would have to be changed to gain a competitive edge.

The second decision concerned how to do it and, particularly, how much risk to take in each instance. This was a tricky decision, balancing (at the least) technological and marketing risks. It was also a critical decision because it determined timing. As he and Brad had agreed the other day, the widespread availability of technology and the proliferation of multiple approaches to meet market needs had put a premium on the appropriate timing. And it was becoming increasingly difficult to sit on a technological lead.

The final decision concerned when to stop and when to redirect projects. The work and preparation necessary to make the first two decisions properly would, of course, really help them all to review each project's progress from the standpoint of its continued strategic significance. Nevertheless, decisions to cut off projects were notoriously tough to make—and making them stick sometimes even tougher. He knew how difficult it was to factor in the opportunity costs of continuing to commit scarce technological resources to projects that had lost their relevance or chance for success. Too often, he knew, investments in ego turned out to be the controlling factor in letting projects continue.

The steps he had already taken were, of course, aimed at forcing these decisions on top management, but he knew he was asking a great deal of some of his executives and he was unsure whether all of them were able to change. There would be a powerful tendency, reinforced by the sheer magnitude of the task, to slip back into the habit of pushing numbers instead of coming to grips with technological and competitive realities.

Has Diversified become too diversified to manage as a single profit center? he wondered. *If so, I'll have to bring more top management focus on particular products or markets. Or maybe the company should slow down its diversification until the executives learn how to manage it better.* That was one reason Miles had alluded in his memo to some possible further moves.

But Miles was most concerned about the company's attitude toward change, as reflected by its top management. *If the signals coming from the top pointed so clearly to an ultraconservative technological strategy, what else could I expect from the down-the-line people? There are bound to be a few innovative souls out there, not all of them in Jim Pasinaro's department.* But the evidence of the past two weeks had shaken him.

I suppose that to an independent observer DMC has been as much a hotbed of innovation as the Catholic Church or the railroads. Well, that's my problem. Even if it means knocking some heads together, I've got to create a positive attitude toward change. And I will.

He had finished his cigar. He made a note to himself to send a box of Macanudos to Brad first thing in the morning.

New worlds of computer-mediated work

Information technology can radically alter the ways employees approach their tasks and offer managers a chance to develop new approaches to work organization

Shoshana Zuboff

When managers make changes in the ways employees perform their work it's only natural for the employees to resist. Managers themselves are famous for the not-invented-here syndrome that is a disguised way of resisting change. It's not surprising that when they hear about resistance to working with the new information technology managers dismiss it as normal and to be expected. The author of this article maintains that managers should heed the resistance, however, because it is telling them something about the quality of the changes that are taking place. Computer-mediated work is more abstract and can demand new conceptual skills while deemphasizing the importance of direct experience. Information technology can potentially depersonalize supervision, alter social communities, and often means that technology absorbs much of the judgment that routine jobs used to entail. The author suggests ways that managers can use the new technology as an opportunity to re-envision job responsibilities and develop new approaches to the problems of supervision.

Ms. Zuboff is assistant professor of organizational behavior and human resource management at the Harvard Business School. She has consulted with numerous companies on the effects of the computer at work. Her present research is funded by NIMH The Center for Work and Mental Health, with additional support from the Division of Research at the Harvard Business School.
Illustrations by Robert Pryor.

Reprint 82513

One day, in the 1860s, the owner of a textile mill in Lowell, Massachusetts posted a new set of work rules. In the morning, all weavers were to enter the plant at the same time, after which the factory gates would be locked until the close of the work day. By today's standards this demand that they arrive at the same time seems benign. Today's workers take for granted both the division of the day into hours of work and nonwork and the notion that everyone should abide by a similar schedule. But, in the 1860s, the weavers were outraged by the idea that an employer had the right to dictate the hours of labor. They said it was a "system of slavery," and went on strike.

Eventually, the owner left the factory gates open and withdrew his demands. Several years later, the mill owner again insisted on collective work hours. As the older form of work organization was disappearing from other plants as well, the weavers could no longer protest.

In general, industrialization presented people with a fundamental challenge to the way they had thought about behavior at work. The employer's desire to exploit the steam engine as a centralized source of power, coupled with the drive to closely supervise workers and increase the pace of production, resulted in a greater degree of collectivization and synchronization in the workplace. Employers imposed an exact discipline on workers that required them to use their bodies in specified ways in relation to increasingly complex forms of equipment. By the early 1900s, "scientific management" had given supervisors a systematic way to measure and control the worker's body.

Although most workers have accepted the work behavior that industrialization fashioned, the issues behind the New England weavers' resistance lie at the heart of modern labor-management relations. Using collective bargaining, later generations of workers have developed elaborate grievance procedures and work rules that carefully limit an employer's right to control a worker's body.

New forms of technology inevitably change the ways people are mobilized to work as well as the kinds of skills and behavior that are critical for productivity. These changes are rarely born without pain and conflict—nor do they emerge exactly as planners envision them. Instead, new conceptions of work organization and behavior emerge from an interaction between the demands of a new technology, its social organization, and the responses of the men and women who must work with the new technological systems.

In this regard, the weavers' example is doubly instructive. First, it illustrates that during a period of technological transition people are most likely to be aware of and articulate about the quality of the change they are facing. When people feel that the demands a new technology makes on them conflict with their expectations about the workplace, they are likely, during the initial stage of adaptation, to resist. Many managers maintain that employees are simply denying change when they cling to familiar patterns and complain as these forms of sustenance are threatened. But resistance can also reveal an eloquent appraisal of the *quality* of change—a subtle commentary that goes beyond a stubborn attachment to custom.

Second, the weavers' example shows that as a major technological transition recedes into the past, and with it the sense of psychological crisis, older sensibilities tend to become subsumed or repressed. However, original sources of resistance, if they are not properly resolved, can continue to influence the management-labor agenda for many years, even though employees may accommodate the demands of a new technology.

Business is now witnessing a period of technological change that shares some important features with the first industrial revolution. Information technology is rapidly reorganizing the kind of work people do across industries and organizational strata. It is affecting clerical workers through the automation of high-volume back-office operations as well as with word processing and electronic mail. Managers are more frequently making use of computer conferencing, decision-support systems, sophisticated modeling procedures, and new on-line management information systems. Blue-collar workers are increasingly required to interact with computer technology in order to monitor and control a variety of manufacturing and continuous-process operations. During the past year, business people bought one million data terminals, worth $2.6 billion, to supplement the four million terminals already in use. The market for intelligent terminals is expected to grow 25% annually during the coming decade.

This increased use of information technology is altering the technological infrastructure of the workplace. More and more, production in office and factory depends on the computer and large-scale information systems that can control increasingly complex sets of data. And just as with industrial technology, people who are required to use information systems often resist their introduction. When managers allow employee discontent with new computer-based technology a voice, they can learn a great deal about the more subtle effects of this technology and the issues that are likely to challenge their practices in the coming decade.

During the last few years I interviewed approximately 200 employees, supervisors, professionals, and managers from several different organizations in three countries to discover how people at distinct organizational levels respond to their work when it has been fundamentally reorganized by information technology. (See the ruled insert on page 110 for a description of the organizations and their information systems.) In this article, I outline the principal themes that emerged repeatedly from my interviews and observations, both as they pertain to employees' experiences of information systems and as observable, often unintended, consequences for the organization. Finally, I identify some of the implications of these findings for human resource management policies.

Management policies toward automation

In many ways, management policies can determine the effectiveness of automation and the quality of the workplace culture that emerges. In this regard, my discussions with employees and managers reveal two primary concerns.

Substitution & deskilling of labor

The purpose of the intelligent technology at the core of a computer system is to substitute algorithms or decision rules for individual judgments. This substitution makes it possible to formalize the skills and know-how intrinsic to a job and integrate them into a computer program. As decision rules become more explicit, the more they are subject to planning, and the less they require a person to make a decision at each stage of execution. For some jobs the word "decision" no longer implies an act of human judgment, but an information processing activity that occurs according to rules embedded in a computer program.

At present, most programmed decision making has been limited to the most routine jobs in an organization such as high-volume operations where tasks can be simplified and rationalized to maximize outputs and minimize skill requirements. For example, partly by limiting a collector's discretion regarding how or in what order he or she should work on an account, an automated collection system makes it possible to increase production goals and reduce the time spent on each account.

Thus for that activity the key to revenue generation becomes volume instead of collection skills. Collection managers I interviewed believe that the system enables them to recoup more funds while reducing their dependence on skilled collectors. One collection manager described the value of the system:

"It gives us a tighter lock on the collector, and we can hire less skilled people. But there's a real loss to the job of skills and know-how. You are being told what to do by the machine."

But job deskilling is not exclusive to the most routine jobs in the organization. A decision-support system installed for a bank's 20 credit analysts was supposed to free them from the most mechanical and boring aspects of the job. Six months after the system was in place, not a single analyst had used it. As one analyst explained it, "I think, then I write down my calculations directly. I know the company and the problem. With this system, I am supposed to type into the machine and let it think. Why should I let it do my thinking for me?"

Automation of managerial assumptions

Information systems can embody management's assumptions and values about its employees, especially about their commitment and motivation. The automated collection system provides an example of how this happens.

Bill Smith had managed collection activities for 30 years, and management considered his perspective invaluable. In creating the system, designers spent long hours debriefing Smith, and he helped them make many important design decisions. Senior managers explain key design decisions by saying: "We tried to build Bill Smith's brain into the computer. If we did not build it into the system, we might lose to the competition."

When I talked to Bill Smith, some of the reasons the system eliminated most discretion from the job became clear. As Smith put it:

"I like to see people work. I'm a good worker. I don't like to see people take time off. I don't do it."

The depth of memory and extent of communications that computer systems are capable of mean that managerial biases can surround the employee as never before. The cost of Smith's managerial assumptions in the collections operations system was high. A year after the system was in place, turnover had reached almost 100%, and the corporate personnel and employee counseling offices were swamped with complaints from replacements. The new and less-educated collectors presented a different set of problems for management and training. Even with the new staff, turnover remained about three times higher than in the rest of the back-office organization.

Computer mediation of work

As the Bill Smith example illustrates, managerial assumptions can easily get embedded in information systems. But what impact do the new systems have on the organization of work and what actually happens to the people who interact with them?

Work becomes abstract

When information technology reorganizes a job, it fundamentally alters the individual's relation to the task. I call the new relationship "computer mediated." Usually, this means that a person accomplishes a task through the medium of the information system, rather than through direct physical contact with the object of the task.

Computer mediation can be contrasted to other forms of task relationships in terms of the way in which one *knows* about the object of the task. The potter who turns a pot with his or her own hands has direct experience of the task's object through continual series of sights and tactile sensations. These sensations form the basis for moment-by-moment judgments regarding the success of the process and any alterations that the potter should make. Machines, such as a press or a welding torch, usually remove the worker as the direct source of energy for the labor process, but leave the task's object within sensuous range. Those who work with paper and pencil usually feel "in touch" with the objects of their tasks through the activity of writing and because they are the sources of what they write.

With computer-mediated work, employees get feedback about the task object only as symbols through the medium of the information system. Very often, from the point of view of the worker, the object of the task seems to have disappeared "behind the screen" and into the information system.

The distinction in feedback is what separates the linotype machine operator from the clerical worker who inputs cold type, the engineer who works with computer-aided design from one who directly handles materials, the continuous process operator who reads information from a visual display unit from one who actually checks vat levels, and even the bill collector who works with an on-line, real-time system from a predecessor who handled accounts cards. The distinctiveness of computer-mediated work becomes more clear when one contrasts it against the classic image of work from the nineteenth century in which labor was considered to be the transformation of nature by human muscle. Computer-mediated work is the electronic manipulation of symbols. Instead of a sensual activity, it is an abstract one.

Many employees I spoke to reported feeling frustrated because in losing a direct experience of their task it becomes more difficult to exercise judgment over it. In routine jobs, judgment often becomes lodged in the system itself. As one bill collector said:

"In our old system, come the end of the month, you knew what you were faced with. With the automated system, you don't know how to get in there to get certain accounts out. You have to work the way the system wants you to."

People in even more complex jobs can also lose direct experience of their tasks. The comptroller of a bank that was introducing information systems to a variety of functions commented:

"People become more technical and sophisticated, but they have an inferior understanding of the banking business. New people become like systems people and can program instructions that don't necessarily reflect the spirit of the operation."

The auditor at one bank is working with a new information system that frees him from traveling to regional branches. The branches feed financial data directly into the information system that he can access in real time. He described his job this way:

"The job of auditing is very different now. More imagination is required. I am receiving data on-line. I don't go to the branches if I don't want to. I don't see any books. What do I audit in this situation? I always have to be thinking about what is in the system. I may be auditing, but it doesn't feel like it."

The auditor now has access to a new level of complexity in his data. He has the possibility

The research sites

The data reported in this article are principally based on research in three kinds of organizations – banking, retail, and consumer goods. Each of these applications had been in place from six months to one year before I began the interviews.

The information systems in the bank included: **1** a decision-support system in the credit analysis department that was able to perform "routine" calculations for analysts; **2** information systems for account officers that provided overviews and analyses of account activity in relation to the key business criteria of a company; **3** information systems that converted front-end processes such as foreign exchange, letter of credit, and current accounts to an on-line real-time basis, thus altering the work of both back-office employees and a range of managers.

The retail application was the automation of collections activities in the back office of a large discount store chain. Before automation, collectors functioned as entrepreneurs, each with an individual tray of accounts to be collected. The automated system pooled all accounts that were then automatically queued in order of priority and randomly distributed among collectors each day.

In the consumer goods organizations, professionals and managers coordinated and communicated their activities through the use of computer conferencing and electronic mail.

---

of comparing branches according to criteria of his choice and searching out new relationships in the data. But in order to do this, he must now develop a theory of the auditing process. He needs to have a conceptual framework that can guide him through the mass of available information. Theoretical insight and imagination will be the keys to his effectiveness on the job.

By creating a medium of work where imagination instead of experience-based judgment is important, information technology challenges old procedures. Judging a given task in the light of experience thus becomes less important than imagining how the task can be reorganized based on new technical capabilities. In the banking industry, for example, planners are not automating the old, but inventing the new.

While working through information systems seems to require a more challenging form of mental effort, it can also induce feelings of frustration and loss of control.

A collections supervisor described the difference between the manual and computer systems:

"If you work with a manual system and you want to see an account on a given day, you have a paper file and you simply go to that particular section and pull out the file. When you're on the computer system, in a sense all your accounts are kind of floating around in space. You can't get your hands on them."

Some people cope with this frustration by creating physical analogues for their tasks. In one bank branch, an on-line system had been installed to update information on current accounts. Instead of making out tickets that would be sent to a data center for overnight keypunching, operators enter data directly into terminals; the system continuously maintains account information. Despite senior management's efforts to persuade them to change, the branch manager and his staff continued to fill out the tickets. When asked why, they first mentioned the need for a backup system. The real reason came out when the branch manager made the following comment: "You need something you can put your hands on. How else can we be sure of what we are doing?"

People are accustomed to thinking of jobs that require employees to use their brains as the most challenging and rewarding. But instead, the computer mediation of simple jobs can create tasks that are routine and unchallenging, while demanding focused attention and abstract comprehension. Nevertheless, the human brain is organized for action. Abstract work on a mass scale seems likely to create conditions that are peculiar if not stressful to many people. While it does seem that those who shift from conventional procedures to computer-mediated work feel this stress most acutely, it's impossible to forecast what adaptation to the abstraction of work will do to people over the long term.

Social interaction is affected

Doubtless, once information technology reorganizes a set of jobs, new patterns of communication and interaction become possible. In time, these patterns are likely to alter the social structure of an organization.

When resources are centered in the information system, the terminal itself can become employees' primary focus of interaction. This focus can lead people to feel isolated in an impersonal situation. For example, because functional operations in the back office of one bank have been reorganized, a clerical worker can complete an entire operation at his or her "professional" work station, rather than repeat a single procedure of it before passing the item on to someone else. Although employees I talked to were split in their attitudes toward the new back-office system, most of them agreed that it created an uncomfortable isolation. Because they had few remaining reasons to interact with co-workers, the local social network was fragmented.

Decades of research have established the importance of social communities in the workplace and the lengths to which people will go to establish and maintain them. Since people will not easily give up the pleasures of the workplace community, they tend to see themselves at odds with the new technology that transforms the quality of work life. The comments of one employee illustrate this point:

"I never thought I would feel this way, but I really do not like the computer. If a person makes a mistake, dealing with the computer to try and get that mistake corrected is so much red tape. And it's just taken a lot of feeling out of it. You should have people working with people because they are going to give you what you want, and you're going to get a better job all around."

In a very different kind of application, professionals and managers in the R&D organization of a large consumer goods company find the range of their interaction greatly extended with computer conferencing. While there is some evidence of reduced face-to-face interaction, the technology makes it relatively easy to initiate dialogues and form coalitions with people in other parts of the corporation. Clearly, information technology can offset social life in a variety of ways. It is important to realize, however, that this technology has powerful consequences for the structure and function of communication and social behavior in an organization.

New possibilities for supervision & control

The dream of the industrial engineer to create a perfectly timed and rationalized set of activities has never been perfectly realized. Because face-to-face supervision can be carried on only on a partial basis, employees usually find ways to pace their own activities to meet standards at a reasonable rate. Thus, traditionally, supervision depended on the quality of the relationship between supervisor and worker. If the relationship is a positive one, employees are likely to produce quality work without constant monitoring. If the relationship is adversarial, the monitoring will be continual.

But because work accomplished through the medium of video terminals or other intelligent equipment can be recorded on a second-by-second basis, the industrial engineer's presence can be built into all real-time activities. With immediate access to how much employees are producing through printouts or other visual displays, supervisors and managers can increase surveillance without depending on face-to-face supervision. Thus the interpersonal relationship can become less important to supervision than access to information on the quality and quantity of employee output. One bank supervisor described this new capability:

"Instead of going to someone's desk and physically pulling out files, you have the ability to review peoples' work without their knowledge. So I think it keeps them on their toes."

Another variant of remote supervision involves controls that are automatically built into systems operations, as in the collections system described earlier. These rules are substitutes for a certain amount of supervisory effort. Because the system determines what accounts the collector should work on and in what order, a supervisor does not have to monitor collectors' judgments on these issues. Managers also see automatic control as the organization's defense against the potentially massive pollution of data that can occur through access by many people to an on-line real-time system.

Remote supervision, automatic control, and greater access to subordinates' information all become possible with computer-mediated work. In some cases, these capabilities are an explicit objective, but too often management employs them without sufficiently considering the potential human and organizational consequences.

With remote supervision, many employees limit their own risk-taking behavior, such as spotting an error in the data and correcting it, developing a more effective approach to the work than the procedures established by the information system, or trying to achieve quality at the expense of keeping up with new production standards.

One reason the initiative to design a custom-made approach to a particular task has become too risky is that many people have difficulty articulating why their approach might be superior to other alternatives. Usually, management has developed a clearly articulated model of the particular task in order to automate it, and if employees cannot identify their own models with equal clarity, they have little hope of having their views legitimated.

Another reason for decreased employee initiative is that the more an information system can control the details of the job, the less even relatively trivial risk-taking opportunities are available. Finally, the monitoring capabilities increase the likelihood that a supervisor will notice a deviation from standard practice. As one bank employee noted:

"Sometimes I have a gut feeling I would rather do something another way. But, because it is all going to be in the computer, it changes your mind. If somebody wouldn't listen to the reason why you did it that way, well, it could cause you quite a problem."

Another frequent response to the new relationships of supervision and control involves perceptions of authority in the workplace. Employees can tend to see technology less as an instrument of authority than as a source of it. For instance, one group of bank employees with an especially easygoing manager described the work pace on their computer-mediated jobs as hard-driving, intense, and at times unfair, but thought the manager was friendly, relaxed, and fair-minded.

One collector told about the difference in her attitudes toward her work under the manual system and under the automated system:

"When I worked with the account cards, I knew how to handle my responsibilities. I felt, 'Hey! I can handle this!' Now I come in every day with a defeatist attitude, because I'm dealing with the tube every day. I can't beat it. People like to feel not that they are necessarily ahead of the game, but that they have a chance. With the tube I don't have a chance."

While this employee knows that her manager is the actual authority in the office, and that he is in turn accountable to other managers, she has an undeniable feeling that the system, too, is a kind of authority. It is the system she must fight, and, if she wins, it is the system she vanquishes.

In the Volvo plant in Kalmar, Sweden, a computer system was installed to monitor assembly operations.[1] A feedback device was programmed to flash a red light signalling a quality control problem. The workers protested against the device, insisting that the supervisory function be returned to a foreman. They preferred to answer to a human being with whom they could negotiate, argue, and explain rather than to a computer whose only means of "communication" was unilateral. In effect, they refused to allow the computer to become, at least in this limited situation, an authority. Yet clearly, the issue would never have arisen in the first place were the technology not capable of absorbing the characteristics of authority.

Finally, these capacities of information systems can do much to alter the relationships among managers themselves. A division or plant manager can often leverage a certain amount of independence by maintaining control of key information. Though a manager might have to present the data in monthly or quarterly reports, he or she has some control over the amount and format. With information technology, however, senior managers in corporate headquarters increasingly have access to real-time systems that display the day-to-day figures of distinct parts of the company's business. For instance, a division vice president can be linked to the information system that transmits raw production data from a processing plant in another state. Such data can provide the vice president with a view of the plant that only the plant manager or mid-level managers in the operation previously had.

This new access raises several questions for a corporation. First, some policy decisions must be confronted that address the kind of information appropriate to each level of management. Top managers can quickly find themselves inundated with raw data that they do not have the time to understand. It also creates a tendency for top managers to focus on the past and present when they should be planning the future.

It would seem that this new access capability would expand top management's opportunities to monitor and direct and, therefore, improve the performance of subordinate managers. But as the on-line availability of such information reaches across management hierarchies (in some companies all the way to board chairpersons), reduced risk taking and its effects begin to take hold. Managers are reluctant to make decisions on the basis of information that their superiors receive simultaneously. As one plant manager said to his boss in division headquarters: "I'm telling you, Bob, if you're going to be hooked up to the data from the pumps, I'm not going to manage them anymore. You'll have to do it."

Birth of the information environment

Another consequence of information technology is more difficult to label, but its effects are undeniable. I call it the "information environment." It refers to a quality of organizational life that emerges when the computer mediates jobs and begins to influence both horizontal and vertical relationships. In the information environment, people generally have greater access to data and, in particular, data relevant to their own decision making. The capacity for follow-up and reorganizing increases as information retrieval and communication can occur with greater ease and convenience than ever before.

One effect of this immediate access to information is a rise in the volume of transactions or operations. This increase, in turn, compresses time and alters the rhythm of work. While people were once satisfied if a computer system responded in 24 hours, those who work with computers now are impatient if information takes more than five seconds to appear. Timely and reliable functioning of the system determines workers' output, and these effects extend up the managerial ladder. Once managers become accustomed to receiving in two hours a report that once took two weeks to compile, they will consider any delay a burden. This speed of access, retrieval, and information processing is allegedly the key to improving the productivity of the organization, but few organizations have seriously considered the appropriate definition of productivity in their own operations. In the meantime, more transactions, reports, and infor-

1 "Social Effects of Automation," International Federation of Automated Control Newsletter, No. 6, September 1978.

mation are generated in an ever-shorter amount of time.

Responses to the information environment usually are accompanied by feelings about power and orderliness. To some people, the increased access to information enhances their power over the contingencies of their work. An account officer for one bank states:

"I never had such a complete picture of a particular customer before. I can switch around the format of the base for my reporting purposes and get a full picture of where the bank is making money. This gives me a new power and effectiveness in my work."

While most people agree that the information environment makes the workplace more orderly, responses to this orderliness tend to be bipolar. Some see the order as "neat and nice," while others perceive it as increasing the regimentation of the workplace. Responses of two collections managers illustrate these differences. The first described the system this way:

"The computer simply alleviates a lot of paperwork. Everything is lined up for you instead of you having to do it yourself. If you are sloppy, the system organizes you."

Another manager in the same organization regards the collections system in a different way:

"Things were a lot more relaxed before the tubes. Before, you scheduled your day yourself; now the machine lines it up for you. This means a more rigid environment because we can track things better."

Greater regimentation can also affect the environment of the professional. A vice president in one organization where professionals have come to rely heavily on electronic mail and computer conferencing puts it this way:

"I used to make notes to myself on things I had to follow up. Now those notes go into my electronic mail system. The system automatically tracks these things and they are there in front of me on the screen if I haven't followed up yet. Nothing slips through the cracks, but certainly for the way professionals usually operate, it's more regimented."

Many of the managers and professionals I talked to are wary of systems that seem to encroach on their judgment, their freedom, or the "artistry" of their professional assessments. Instead of feeling that increased information augments their power, these people resist information systems that they see limiting their freedom or increasing the measurability of their work.

At present, most professionals and managers function in fairly ambiguous environments. Information is imperfectly exchanged (often in corridors, washrooms, or over lunch), and considerable lag time usually occurs before the quality of decisions can be assessed. A continual flow of complete information, however, reduces ambiguity. For example, in the marketing area of one bank, an information system provides complete profiles of all accounts while it assesses their profitability according to corporate criteria. Top management and systems developers believed the system could serve as a constant source of feedback to account officers and senior managers, allowing them to better manage their account activities and maximize fee-based revenues. But some bankers saw the flow of "perfect" information as not only reducing ambiguity but also limiting their opportunities for creative decisions and resisted using it.

Limited information may create uncertainty in which people make errors of judgment, but it also provides a "free space" for inspiration. This free space is fundamental to the psychology of professional work. The account officers in the bank had traditionally been motivated by the opportunity to display their artistry as bankers, but as increased information organizes the context of their work, the art in their jobs is reduced.

Employees in back-office clerical jobs also tend to perceive the increased time and volume demands and the measurability of operations as limits on their opportunities to experience a sense of mastery over the work. To overcome these effects, many of the collectors keyed fictitious data into the system of account files. Their managers were confronted with high productivity figures that did not match the size of monthly revenues.

Many managers first respond to such a situation by searching out ways to exert more control over the work process. I am convinced that the more managers attempt to control the process, the more employees will find ways to subvert that control. This response is particularly likely when outsmarting the system becomes the new ground on which to develop and test one's mastery. Managers may dismiss these subversive activities as "resistance to change," but in many cases this resistance is the only way employees can respond to the changes they face. Such resistance can also be understood as a positive phenomenon—it is evidence of an employee's identification with the job.

Listening to the resistance

Critics of technology tend to fall into one of three camps. Some bemoan new developments and see them as a particular form of human debasement and depersonalization. Others are ready to applaud any form of technology as progress toward

some eventual conquest of dumb nature. Finally, others argue that technology is neutral and its meaning depends on the uses to which human beings press its application. I have found none of these views sufficient.

It is true that information technology provides a particularly flexible set of technical possibilities, and thus can powerfully embody the assumptions and goals of those whom it is designed to serve. Yet, while the value and meaning of a given application must be read, in part, from management's intentions, beliefs, and commitments, this does not imply the ultimate neutrality of the technology itself. To say that information technology is neutral is like saying an airplane is neutral because it can fly to either Washington or Moscow. We know that airplanes are not neutral because we all live in a world that has been radically altered by the facts of air travel—the globe has been shrunk, time and space have collapsed.

If one accepts that technology is *not* neutral, it follows that information technology must have attributes that are unique in the world view they impose and the experience of work to which they give shape. The flexibility, memory, and remote access capabilities of information systems create new management possibilities and, therefore, choices in the design of an application.

This argument suggests three general areas for management deliberation and action in the deployment of new information systems. The first concerns policies that shape the quality of the employment relationship. The second involves attitudes toward managerial control, and the third concerns basic beliefs about the nature of an organization and the role of management.

The quality of the employment relationship

Because the computer mediation of work can have direct consequences for virtually every area of human resource management including skills training, career paths, the social environment, peer relationships, supervision, control, decision making, authority, and organization design, managers need to think through the kind of workplace they want to foster. They need to make design choices that reflect explicit human resource management policies.

For example, consider the automated collections system I described earlier. Although the system minimizes individual decision making, most managers I interviewed in that organization believe that collector skill and judgment are critical variables in the organization's ability to generate payments and have compelling financial data to support that view.

A management policy commitment to maintaining skill levels, providing challenging jobs, and promoting collector loyalty and motivation could have resulted in an information system that preserves the entrepreneurial aspects of the collector's job while rationalizing its administration with on-line record-keeping. But to assess the likely consequences of an approach to automation that strictly rationalizes procedures, managers need to understand the human logic of a job. In many cases, this human logic holds the clue to the motivational aspects of the job that should be preserved in the conversion to new technology.

What do managers do when faced with some of the more intrinsic features of information technology? First, they need to understand the kinds of skill demands that the computer mediation of work generates, and to construct educational programs that allow employees to develop the competencies that are most relevant to the new environment.

If a more theoretical comprehension of the task is required for effective utilization of the information system, then employees should be given the opportunity to develop this conceptual understanding. If an information system is likely to reduce the sense (if not the fact) of individual control over a task, is it possible to redesign the job to reinvest it with a greater self-managing capacity? As elements of supervision and coordination are loaded into jobs that have been partially drained of challenge, new learning and career development opportunities can open up. The astonishing quantity of information that is available can be used to increase employees' feedback, learning, and self-management rather than to deskill and routinize their jobs or remotely supervise them.

New systems are often presented with the intention of providing "information resources" for more creative problem solving. Unless employees are actually given the knowledge and authority to utilize such resources in the service of more complex tasks, these systems will be undermined, either through poor utilization or more direct forms of resistance.

The focus of managerial control

Because of the many self-management opportunities the information resource makes possible, managers may have to rethink some classic notions of managerial control. When industrial work exerted stringent demands on the placement and timing of physical activity, managers focused on controlling bodies and stipulating the precise ways in which they should perform.

With the burgeoning of office work, physical discipline was less important than reading or writing and, above all, interpersonal behavior. Because

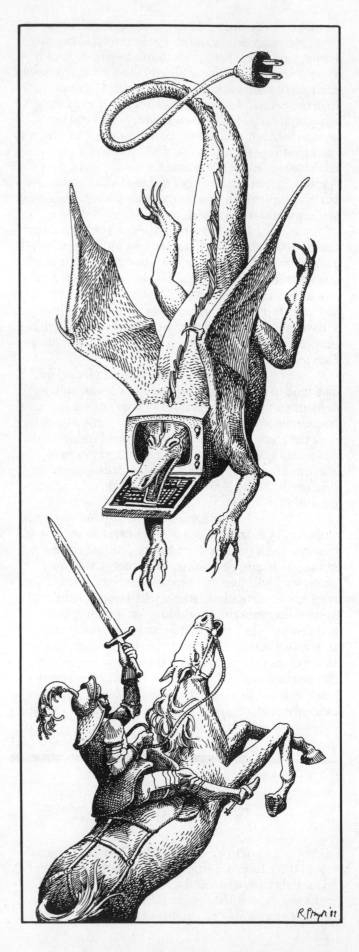

people needed to learn how to behave with superiors, subordinates, and the public, managers began to control less what people did with their bodies and more what they did with one another—their communication, teamwork, meeting behavior, and so forth.

With computer-mediated work, neither physical activity nor interpersonal behavior appear to be the most appropriate targets of managerial control. Instead, patterns of attention, learning, and mental engagement become the keys to effectiveness and high-quality performance. Obviously, people have always had to "pay attention" to their work in order to accomplish it properly. But the quality of attention computer-mediated work requires is essentially different.

For instance, in almost all accounts of routine work, researchers report that employees are daydreaming and bantering with one another while they accomplish their tasks. Of course, they must pay attention with their eyes, but not so much with their brains. In contrast, people concentrating on a visual display unit must pay a very different sort of attention. If employees are to understand and properly respond to information, they must be mentally involved.

Managers can experiment to find how to make the most of people's attending and learning qualities as well as their overall engagement in the information environment. One observation that emerges from my current field research is that imposing traditional supervisory approaches on the computer-mediated environment can create considerable dysfunction. Supervisors and managers who concentrate on the physical and interpersonal behavior of employees working with information systems simply exacerbate tensions instead of creating an environment that nurtures the kind of learning and attention computer-mediated work makes necessary and compensating for some of its less obvious but potentially negative attributes.

The nature of organization & management

With information technology, managers will do a variety of tasks that others once did for them. Because of this, we are likely to see a gradual shift in the overall shape of the organization from a pyramid to something closer to a diamond shape—with a diminishing clerical support staff, swelling numbers of professionals and middle managers, and a continually more remote, elite, policy-making group of senior managers.

While these considerations should be of central importance to management policy in the coming years, as a society we are sure to see a continuing challenge to the salience of work and the workplace in our daily lives. The traditional importance of occupational distinctiveness may be further eroded as what it means to "accomplish a task" undergoes a fundamental change. When a person's primary work consists of monitoring or interacting with a video screen, it may become more difficult to answer the questions, "Who am I?" and "What do I do?" Identification with an occupational role may diminish, while the transferability of on-the-job skills increases. Will this have implications for individual commitment to an organization and for the relative importance of work and nonwork activities?

Information technology is also likely to introduce new forms of collective behavior. When the means of production becomes dependent on electronic technology and information flows, it is no longer inevitable that, as in the case of the weavers, work be either collective or synchronous. As long as a terminal and communications links are available, people will be able to perform work in neighborhood centers, at home, or on the road. At the same time, electronic technology is altering the traditional structure and function of communication within the organization. Who interacts with whom in the organization? Can the neat chain of command hierarchy be maintained? Should it be? What does it take to lead or influence others when communication itself becomes computer mediated? Finally, who is likely to gain or lose as we make the transition to this environment?

These developments make it necessary to rethink basic conceptions of the nature of organization and management. What is an organization if people do not have to come face to face in order to accomplish their work? Does the organization itself become an abstraction? What happens to the shared purpose and commitment of members if their face-to-face interaction is reduced? Similarly, how should an "abstract" organization be managed?

If information technology is to live up to its promise for greater productivity, managers need to consider its consequences for human beings and the qualities of their work environments. The demands for a thoughtful and energetic management response go deeper than the need for a "friendly interface" or "user involvement." The underlying nature of this technology requires understanding; the habitual assumptions used in its design must surface. Managers' ability to meet these demands will be an important determinant of the quality of work in future organizations. ▽